Mysteries of the
CORNISH COAST

*Legends, Ghosts and Extraordinary Events
from Cornwall's South-West Peninsula*

• HALSGROVE DISCOVER SERIES ➤

Mysteries of the
CORNISH COAST

*Legends, Ghosts and Extraordinary Events
from Cornwall's South-West Peninsula*

Ian Addicoat and Geoff Buswell

HALSGROVE

First published in Great Britain in 2003

British Library Cataloguing-in-Publication Data
A CIP record for this title is available from the British Library

ISBN 1 84114 255 7

HALSGROVE

Halsgrove House
Lower Moor Way
Tiverton, Devon EX16 6SS
Tel: 01884 243242
Fax:01884 243325
email: sales@halsgrove.com
website: www.halsgrove.com

Printed by D'Auria Industrie Grafiche Spa, Italy

Contents

Introduction   7

Location of Stories (map)   11

Phantom Ships
Ghostly Ships   13
The Death Ship of St Ives Bay   14
The Sally   15
Cornwall's *Mary Celeste* Stories   17
The Porthcurno Black Rigger   17
The Evil Wrecker of Tregeseal   21

Smugglers and Pirates
The Smugglers' Ghosts   26
Abbey Street, Penzance   27
The Fair Trader of Mullion   29
Pengersick Castle, Praa Sands   34
Screams at Hell's Mouth   36
The Real Pirates of Penzance   39
The Legend of Penrose Manor   44
Spirits at the Inn – The Admiral Benbow, Penzance   50
Spirits at the Inn – The First and Last, Sennen   51

Animal Ghosts
The Cliff Creature, Carbis Bay   53
The Phantom White Horse of St Ives   55
The Black Dog of Penzance Harbour   58
The Daisy Dog   61

Sailors' Spirits

The Newlyn Cottage Ghost   65
The Porthgwarra Sweethearts   67
Pistol Meadow   74
The Seamen's Morgue and Other Ghosts, Portreath   79
Deadman's Cove   82
The Seaman's Ghost of Zennor   83
The Sailor's Ghost, Penzance   87
Spirits at the Inn, The Dolphin Tavern, Penzance   91
The Boatmen of Porthmeor Beach, St Ives   93

Strange Ladies

The Lady and the Lantern, St Ives   95
The Irish Lady   98
Sarah Polgrean (Polgreen), Ludgvan   100
The Grey Lady, St Michael's Mount   108
The Mermaid of Lamorna, Lamorna Cove   111
Lutey and the Mermaid, Berepper Sands   113
The Mermaid of Zennor   115
Madge Figgy, Witch and Wrecker, Land's End   119

Mysterious Cries and Strange Phenomena

The Hooper, Sennen Cove   122
Screams at Battery Rocks, Penzance   125
The Phantom Revellers, Mount's Bay   128
The Captain's Tomb, St Levan   129
Jack Harry's Lights, Cornish Coast   132
The Lost Lands of Lyonesse, Mount's Bay   135
Demon Tregeagle, Loe Bar, Porthcurno   139

Bibliography and Further Reference   143

Introduction

Cornwall, the land of the two peninsulas, Lizard and Penwith, projects into the grey Atlantic Ocean like the talon of a giant claw, lying in wait for unwary vessels to stray into danger. There has been no respite in the making of an unending list of wrecked ships, from earliest times to the present day. Victims of the 'Grey Widow Maker' have either drowned without trace or been torn apart on the razor-sharp rocks of the granite headlands which pierce the Atlantic diorama. Only a few have survived to recount the tragedies to their waiting kin.

On a bright summer's day, in the absence of an onshore breeze, Mount's Bay can take on the appearance of blue carpet, without imperfection, tranquil as a newborn lamb. In the teeth of a force-ten gale during January, with 8-metre waves, the surface of the ocean boils and roars like a raging, unforgiving lion devouring its prey. The English Channel approaches turn white and a snow-storm of spume drenches the granite cliff fortresses with millions of tons of churning salt water.

To understand Cornwall, in particular the remote south-west of Penwith, one cannot possibly ignore the influence of the ocean and the constantly changing weather patterns. The sea has always been central to the Cornish economy, in the past principally for fishing, and in the present era for tourism. The pilchard or 'fair maiden' was the core of nineteenth-century prosperity from fishing, but the industry and its shoreline have also provided an appalling arena for death, terror, countless legends and ghost stories. The Cornish Sea God, the Bucca, could, like the Cornish themselves, be caring, generous and welcoming, but unfortunately this Celtic deity was equally, and without warning, able to raise havoc and tempest, and initiate tragedy.

The Cornish climate, together with its surrounding seas, has for centuries largely governed the pattern of life and death in its region, and the tales which originate from maritime fable would stretch the imagination of any ballad writer. Behold Cornwall's dark brooding cliffs, restless tidal movements, ancient ports and captivating characters, and you have the enchanting stuff of riveting narrative.

On preparing this publication, we discovered a library of tales concerning mysterious strangers, mermaids, lost lands, demons, witches, heroic seafarers, smugglers and wreckers, as well as ghosts and phantoms of every type. Ghosts, it seems, are almost as common as the traditional Cornish pasty and can make an appearance at almost any time to enhance the dominant environmental atmosphere of mystery and magic.

It does not take long to realise the individuality of the county of Cornwall. In many senses, little has changed over the last millennium; even today, struggling across Penwith moors in the face of a winter storm, man's inability to impose radical change on such an open landscape can be witnessed. Often the only signs of habitation, in the form of visible remains, are the rough, walled fields, frequent ancient dolmens and ruined farm buildings which dot the land. It is perhaps this perceived weak grasp of man on his environment which allows the paranormal to encroach more readily into this world of normal experience.

The task to locate the 'best' supernatural stories associated with the coastline of Cornwall has proved to be difficult and a matter of personal selection. In the book's compilation we have attempted to elicit variety, whilst opting to focus on the area of coast between Portreath in the north and Falmouth in the south. This remote area has been a hot spot for supernatural activity over many centuries, but what has caused this region to amass such an apparent concentration of paranormal intrusion?

Perhaps the Cornish have always been a 'nation apart', inhabiting what today is regarded by many Celts as 'an island', almost detached from mainland Britain by the River Tamar and the restless sea. Cornwall boasts of classic legends such as King Arthur and Merlin, Tristan and Iseult, giants, piskies and so many more, as an integral part of its heritage. The area has also suffered from two millennia of constant foreign integration by Romans, Normans, Saxons and others, each wave having influenced the local folk culture. Tales of super-heroes, gods, myths and mysticism have been retold repeatedly around the dancing flames of a crackling fire on a dark winter's night.

How easy it is for the town dweller to discount the odd ghostly tale as just fanciful imagination. Equally, how certain would one be on a black winter's night, facing a howling Atlantic storm and looking down to the rocky shore-line of St Ives Island, only to see a tantalising glimmer of light flitting from place to place? Who could be certain that this sighting was definitely not the poor despairing 'Lady of the Lantern', searching for her lost, drowned baby? Similarly, how sure would the visitor be that the harrowing screams of the seagulls, carried over the storm-tossed Tol-Pedn-Penwith cliff line, were not indeed the crazed cries of Madge Figgy, local witch and merciless wrecker, laughing at shipwreck victims dying on the rocks below?

As you venture into this cocktail of Cornish maritime mysterious tales, remember that West Penwith is widely acknowledged by ghost researchers as the most haunted district in the British Isles, with more paranormal sightings per square kilometre than anywhere else. We sincerely hope that through the following pages we are able to take the reader along a 40-mile stretch of the Cornish coastline and relate the stories in an original way. Therefore, we have broken down each tale into the following format: firstly, to tell the tale as it is commonly known and, if possible, adopt a fresh approach with additional background detail; secondly, ghost-hunting addicts can read about the witnesses to the haunting or supernatural events, both past and present, and have some indication as to the likelihood of actually encountering something for themselves. Comments as to the frequency of such events can help to quantify this for the observer. Finally, where possible, locations have been pinpointed with Ordnance Survey grid references and sketch-maps, enabling the keen walker and amateur ghost sleuth to reach many remote and little-known sites. By making these more accessible, enthusiasts are offered a real 'hands-on approach' to the environmental surrounds and atmosphere.

In conclusion, please remember that ghosts, apparitions and supernatural occurrences do not just appear on demand to amuse the living. You may visit a haunted location many times and experience nothing unusual. It is that one special time – often without warning – when, like us, you may be able to gather strong evidence to sustain the existence of the paranormal. If you are fortunate (or unfortunate!) enough to witness the unexplained, do not expect it to be easy to persuade others of your evidence. Most people fear ridicule and very rarely does any 'self-respecting' ghost leave tangible proof to support your unlikely tale. However, do not let this put you off your quest. If you go to places often enough, are patient, respectful and ever-vigilant, you never know. Good luck! Good reading! Happy hunting!

If you are successful in experiencing the supernatural, either at a location mentioned in this book, or anywhere else, we would appreciate hearing from you.

The greatest care has been taken to identify and locate these stories and places. However, we cannot be responsible for future changes, since the areas can only be described as at the time of writing. One can never know what the future holds, and places are liable to considerable alteration, even those of outstanding beauty. Also, please remember that certain sites may be, or may become, private property. Therefore, please do respect trespass laws and people's rights to privacy. Finally, do respect the Countryside Code and help to preserve the natural beauty of the Cornish landscape. Above all, please take care, do not take risks, do not visit places that are perilous and be extra careful during poor weather conditions. Enjoy Cornwall's coast but make sure you are safe to tell the tale!

Ian Addicoat and Geoff Buswell

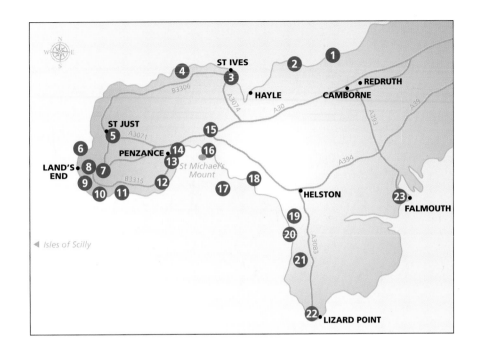

LOCATION OF STORIES

STORY NUMBER

1 The Seamen's Morgue and Other Ghosts, Portreath

2 Screams at Hell's Mouth/Deadman's Cove

3 The Death Ship of St Ives Bay/*The Sally*/The Cliff Creature, Carbis Bay/The Phantom White Horse of St Ives/The Boatmen of Porthmeor Beach/The Lady and the Lantern

4 The Seaman's Ghost of Zennor/The Mermaid of Zennor

5 The Evil Wrecker of Tregeseal

6 The Irish Lady/The Hooper, Sennen Cove

7 The Legend of Penrose Manor

8 The First and Last Inn, Sennen

9 The Daisy Dog/Tregeagle, the Cornish Demon

10 The Porthgwarra Sweethearts/Madge Figgy, Witch and Wrecker/The Captain's Tomb, St Levan

11 The Porthcurno Black Rigger

12 The Mermaid of Lamorna

13 The Newlyn Cottage Ghost

14 Abbey Street, Penzance/The Real Pirates of Penzance/The Admiral Benbow/The Black Dog of Penzance Harbour/The Sailor's Ghost, Penzance/The Dolphin Tavern/Screams at Battery Rocks

15 Sarah Polgrean, Lugvan

16 St Michael's Mount, The Grey Lady

17 Mount's Bay, The Phantom Revellers/Lands of Lyonesse

18 Pengersick Castle, Praa Sands

19 Tregeagle, the Cornish Demon

20 Lutey and the Mermaid

21 The Fair Trader of Mullion

22 Pistol Meadow

23 Cornwall's *Mary Celeste* Stories

Dedication

We would like to dedicate this book to the memory of all the poor unfortunate victims of the Cornish sea coast, who have lost their lives in storm, accident or other tragic circumstances. May they rest in eternal peace.

Phantom Ships

The Death Ship – St Ives Bay
The Sally – St Ives Bay
Cornwall's *Mary Celeste* Stories – Falmouth
The Black Rigger – Porthcurno
The Evil Wrecker – Tregeseal

GHOSTLY SHIPS

There are countless stories about shipwrecks in Cornwall. Over the centuries, disaster has befallen hundreds of hapless vessels, costing the lives of thousands of crew members. Sinister hulks still litter the Cornish coast, sometimes protruding like grim models, to remind us all of the perilous nature of the sea.

Not surprisingly, with such an extended history of tragedy, there are many tales about phantom ships, and ghostly encounters with them, throughout the county. They are often witnessed gliding out of stormy seas as if still on some macabre eternal journey. Many are said to be an omen of doom, not to be tangled with. Without exception they remind people of the risks undertaken by the sailor, fisherman or pleasure-tripper every time they set sail on 'God's' deep ocean.

Many Cornish sailors claim that ships are often haunted by the spirits of drowned seamen. These vessels are considered fortunate, for with such an ethereal shipmate, a ship is unlikely to be wrecked. The ghosts are bound to look out for the boat's safety and give warning of forthcoming storms or other perils to their craft.

THE DEATH SHIP OF ST IVES BAY

One such ship, fitting the profile to perfection, is the ghostly vessel believed to appear sporadically in St Ives Bay. It is a remarkably persistent story, still holding much credence amongst the locals of St Ives today. Some of the many tourists visiting this beautiful town of golden beaches, fishing and art, may wish to quell their scepticism because the ghost ship has appeared all too frequently over the decades. There are two slightly differing versions of the story, but it would appear that each account has come from the same origin.

One version claims that a spectral ship often appears in St Ives Bay as a portent of disaster at sea. In the main, the boat seems to be very real as it slowly drifts across the waters, just off St Ives Island. On several reported occasions, local fishing boats have witnessed the ship and attempted to hail the crew. However, it is not long before they realise they are dealing with a ghost ship. For example, some years ago, a fishing boat was heading towards what appeared to be a ship in trouble to offer assistance. As they drew nearer, the fishermen were shocked to see the whole ship covered in ice, including the deck, masts and sails. Nevertheless, one man volunteered to lean across and try to grasp hold of the ship's bulwarks – only to find he was clutching at thin air. The ship had vanished as if it had been made of mist. Just a few hours later, a ship sailing from London named *Neptune* was tragically wrecked in a ferocious storm at nearby Gwithian. Everybody on board drowned, and it was soon widely believed that the earlier ship was a harbinger of doom. There were even some who claimed that the 'Death Ship' had appeared with a bright light hovering over her deck. This was suggested to be Jack Harry's Lights (see p.132–3).

On another occasion, a pilot boat from St Ives spotted a ship in trouble and headed out to meet her. As they came closer, the crew were horrified as the boat vanished before their eyes. Yet another St Ives crew witnessed the phantom ship of doom years later. This time it actually sailed alongside them for quite some time before vanishing, but not before several ghostly figures were spotted milling around on the deck. Not surprisingly, the men were filled with fear and awe. On most occasions, the ship appears to be completely solid, like a large schooner; at other times transparent and white.

The second version of the story claims that the schooner is the *Neptune* herself and appears at the exact spot where this ship went down in the nineteenth century. It is said to head across the bay firing distress flares and displaying signs of panic aboard. Perhaps, as some have suggested, this spectral transport is still being sailed by the *Neptune*'s famous captain Richard Grant, with him still at the helm, determined this time to lead his crew safely to shore.

St Ives Bay has more than its fair share of tales, allegedly being home to phantom bells which have long sounded out their peculiar chimes. It is also said to possess another phantom ship…

THE SALLY

In 1862 the sloop ship *The Sally* was wrecked off St Ives and Hayle. Ever since that time, in the early hours of the morning, people have frequently claimed that they have witnessed the same ship gliding across the bay in the direction of Hayle. Some claim that two separate fishing boats have headed towards the ship and come close enough to read the name clearly painted on the side and were horrified to read the words *The Sally* before she vanished. Other people claim to have been standing on the wharf in St Ives between midnight and 2am and seen this ghostly sloop.

There is a famous and bizarre tale, rivalling anything from the pen of Bram Stoker. One man had a peculiar experience, claiming he was standing on the wharf when he saw the ghost ship heading out across the bay. Walking across the wharf, he noticed a strange-looking man leaning up against a post, to whom he nodded politely and began to speak. He was slightly perturbed when there was no answer, and was about to walk away when the man began to raise his head and look at him. To the witness's utter revulsion, the man revealed a hideous appearance. The face was ugly, with bulging eyes and his flesh scalded and scarred beyond belief. Even this was not the most terrifying aspect, because there, dangling from the corner of the ghoul's mouth, was a wet piece of seaweed, spilling down from his lips. The poor onlooker had witnessed more than he had bargained for in one evening, and beat a hasty retreat, running down the street. But his terror mounted as soon he heard footsteps following closely behind him all the way along the road. His flesh began to crawl as he heard the definitive noise which accompanied each footstep; squelch, squelch, squelch! Not surprisingly, he sprinted away as fast as he could and eventually came running around the corner. Here he was greeted by his worst nightmare. The same man was standing there ahead of him, with a wide hideous grin etched across his countenance. Unfortunately, the part of the story relating what happened next seems to have been lost…

The tale may sound like complete fantasy. However, it is a very well-known and persistent story.

The Evidence

There have been no sightings recently which can be seriously substantiated. The authors have been unable to find anyone who has witnessed either vessel in the last few years and, not surprisingly, none have encountered the 'seaweed connoisseur'. The last confirmed sighting of a possible phantom ship was about fifteen years ago, by a local fishing crew on their way back from sea, just past St Ives Island. Perhaps a visit is well overdue.

Location

St Ives Bay can be seen most effectively from the Island, though it can also be viewed from most places around St Ives (see directions for 'The Lady and the Lantern' – map p.57).

CORNWALL'S *MARY CELESTE* STORIES

The town of Falmouth, for long an influential port, has a very interesting and true story.

In 1917 a schooner named *Zebrina* departed Falmouth on a short trip to France. The boat was spotted two days later slowly drifting, unmanned. There was no apparent explanation as to why the whole crew had vanished, leaving behind all of their belongings. Indeed, the sails were set for good speed, and the crew's food fully prepared ready for eating. There were no signs of anything wrong, the weather had been perfectly calm; everything appeared otherwise normal. Nevertheless, the disappearance was a mystery never to be solved.

More remarkably, just sixty-eight years earlier, an almost identical event occurred, also off the Cornish coast. In 1849 a ship sailing from Holland, *The Hermania,* was discovered floating off the coast, near the Eddystone lighthouse. Once the ship was boarded a remarkable scene met the men. The schooner was utterly deserted; not a single member of the crew remained, yet everything on board was still in place. Nothing had been removed and the lifeboat was still coupled to the side. Many of the crew's belongings lay around as if they had recently been used. This too was an enigma, perhaps even more difficult to explain than the famous *Mary Celeste*.

THE PORTHCURNO BLACK RIGGER

A ghostly lugger is also said to haunt a small area of water on the Lizard, overlooked by Goonhilly Downs. However, Cornwall's most famous ghost ship must surely be 'The Black Rigger', found at Porthcurno, near Land's End.

It is believed that Porthcurno was once an impressive port where large ships came to shelter. After a great storm had thrown the sands up, boats were never again able to enter the harbour. Today the village is most famous for the magical Minack Theatre on the cliffs, the Museum of Submarine Telegraphy, and its impressive bay flanked with brooding granite cliffs and golden sand. It is difficult to imagine the place as it once may have been, a busy port bustling with ships and activity. At least, that is, unless you bear witness to an extraordinary spectacle. It is claimed that phantom ships can sometimes be spotted just off Porthcurno, sailing up and down mysteriously. These, too, are believed to be portentous, said to warn of impending storms and rough seas. Some believe that the number of tall ships seen will predict exactly how many will be lost during the storm.

When mists are rising, the ghostly black rigger is said to come in from the sea and glide up over the sands, then carry on inland, forewarning of misfortune ahead. This story almost certainly harks back to the legend of the 'Ghost Ship of Porthcurnow', and there are various, slightly differing versions, this being the most enduring.

It is claimed that in the eighteenth century there was a farmhouse at Chegwidden (Chygwiden), a mile or so from the coast, which was the home of a man widely regarded as a cantankerous fellow. He had acquired a very young second wife, who, it was told, was extremely unpleasant towards the man's children from his first marriage, particularly the eldest son, Martin, even though he was older than her. Eventually, the young man had endured quite enough and went to sea. After several years he had failed to return and it was presumed that he must have died.

After many years, all of the original family had passed away, leaving the house and the farm in the care of two relatives, a young man and his sister, Eleanor.

In the course of time Martin returned to Chygwiden, with a mysterious dark - skinned companion named José, and was soon recognised as the true heir to the property. However, he also fell foul of many of the locals, who believed him to be a vile fellow. Whether justified or not, Martin certainly fostered a sinister reputation, though, strangely for one so apparently corrupt, he made no claims on his rightful property and allowed his relatives to continue to own the farm. His odd countenance and undesirable behaviour made him the target for much of the local gossip and he was described as a heavy drinker, big spender and wild huntsman. The rumour was that he and José were pirates, based on the fact that they kept a large ship at Porthcurno and often went to sea for long stretches. It was said they would even set sail during the roughest of storms, yet had an uncanny ability to return unscathed. 'Perhaps they were in league with the Devil,' some suggested. Locals avoided them for fear that they might be party to witchcraft, but it seems Martin and José cared nothing for this treatment. The only person who seemed to like the supposed scoundrels was Eleanor, and the three seemed to be extremely attached.

Ultimately, their hard living must have taken its toll on Martin. He became ill and, after a short time, died. His coffin was laid out in St Levan church, though nobody attended to it and few came to his funeral when the coffin was subsequently buried in St Levan churchyard. Soon the locals were suggesting that something underhand was occurring. Indeed, many suspected that Martin was not inside the coffin at all. Suspicions increased when soon after the burial José was seen dragging heavy boxes on to their ship. Later he set sail and headed out of Porthcurno for the last time, taking with him Eleanor and Martin's beloved dog. At that moment, a powerful storm blew up and lasted for several days. It was said that this was when so much sand was thrown over Porthcurno by the tempest that nobody was ever able to enter again by boat.

The fate of José and his ship and the unknown cargo was never revealed. They were not seen again, though many presumed they must have been drowned.

Soon after the storm had abated, a strange ship was witnessed, just off Porthcurno. Nobody could be sure, but many were convinced it was José and Martin's ghostly vessel, slowly drifting across the bay. On many occasions since, people have claimed that a phantom ship appears near Porthcurno and slowly glides towards the sands. There, as already described, it continues up

PORTHCURNO COVE: This popular tourist beach is the apparent location of the phantom black rigger, seen at sea, before moving up the beach and inland towards Chygwiden (Chegwidden).

on to the beach, and heads across the sand. It then moves up the valley, drifting eerily onwards all the way to Chygwiden. There it is said to hover briefly, before continuing towards the position of the farmhouse and vanishing near a large rock. It was said that many years after this first appearance, people dug under the rock and discovered a large cache of treasure. Perhaps this was the lost fortune accumulated by the mysterious friends during their travels at sea.

The Evidence

There are those today who still claim the phantom barque occasionally can be seen gliding, shrouded in mist and moving along its ghostly route. On clear days people have claimed to glance up to see something peculiar on the deck. The ghostly forms of two men, a young woman and a dog have been observed. They are, of course, assumed to be Martin, José, Eleanor and their beloved dog. This too is said to bring bad luck to those unfortunate enough to witness the spectacle.

Location

Porthcurno (SW388223): Follow the A30 from Penzance to Land's End, turn left at the village of Catchall on to the B3283 and continue on the B3315 to Trethewey. Follow the road left to Porthcurno. (You can also follow the brown signs to Minack Theatre, much of the way.) Chegwidden is situated on the other side of Trethewey (SW381241).

THE EVIL WRECKER OF TREGESEAL

There is a marvellous tale concerning the region around Cape Cornwall and St Just. It contains all the measured ingredients of a classic romance, with phantom ships, wreckers and large 'helpings' of the supernatural.

Several centuries ago, one mild autumn evening, a pirate ship, flying the skull and crossbones, rounded Land's End and then sailed close to the coastline, heading towards Cape Cornwall (topped at present with its tall mine ventilation chimney). The terrified villagers of St Just watched from their sheer granite coastline as the vessel anchored, and a rowing boat, containing a crew, was launched towards Priest's Cove at the Cape. As the boat landed on the shore, they could make out that one of its occupants was in chains. Immediately that his guards removed the manacles, the man broke away, fighting to escape his captors. Eventually he was subdued in deep water, dragged ashore again, screaming wildly, and was then seen to race up and down the beach like a madman.

At this the pirate crew turned tail and rowed quickly back to the waiting ship. The man left on the beach was a strange fellow and many of the locals were disheartened to learn that he had decided to settle in a small cottage in

Tregeseal which was situated nearer the larger village (now town) of St Just. Many of the local residents believed the newcomer to be so evil and wicked that even his fellow pirates had refused him quarter on their ship. Sure enough, before long the Tregeseal pirate had raised a gang of heavies and become their vicious leader. Their favourite pastime was to lure ships on to the rocky shore to be wrecked, by walking along the cliff path with several horses all laden with lanterns. The lights were tied to the animals' heads and the ships' lookouts, in poor visibility, would read these as the stern lights of other ships taking shelter from a storm's fury, close to the shore. By moving into what was seen as a safe haven, the wooden vessels would be torn to pieces on the reefs and their cargoes pilfered from the sea by these murderous wreckers. The Tregeseal gang despatched any survivors swept on to the shore and were said to swiftly hack off the hands of those struggling on the rocks to gain a grip, although most would already have drowned in the ferocious sea.

One autumn day, the Tregeseal villagers were labouring in a barley field near Cape Cornwall, when they heard a loud voice carried on the wind saying, 'The time is come, but the man has not come.' A fierce storm immediately blew up and a black square-rigged sailing ship came into view, moving directly towards the Cape against prevailing wind and tide. The vessel anchored under the cliff at Cape Cornwall. No members of the crew were to be seen on board. The sky over the ship was filled with black, ominous clouds, although elsewhere the sun shone brightly.

The farm labourers fled from the fields to their Tregeseal village. A large crowd had now gathered outside the wrecker's house and they learnt that he had been struck down with an illness. A local priest was summoned to pray for the wrecker's soul, in an attempt to eject the Devil, which was clearly inside him. The man screamed and writhed in his bed, claiming that the Devil was tearing at him with huge talons, whilst he cursed the priest and his fisherman companions. At length, it was claimed that the holy man had succeeded in exorcising the Devil from his victim but not in evicting the demon from the cottage itself. The wrecker's deathbed was soon bathed in an eerie light and the storm centred over the house. Peals of thunder, flashes of lightning and the sound of crashing waves, carried on howling winds, terrified the surrounding onlookers who fled for shelter. The dramatic and frightening tempest unleashed its fury over Tregeseal for some time. Then all of a sudden, the black clouds began to move back towards Cape Cornwall and hovered over the mysterious sailing barque. Eventually both the boat and the clouds vanished into a haze over the sea.

The priest and locals returned to the wrecker's house to find him stone-cold dead in his bed, with a look of sheer terror fixed in his staring eyes. A coffin was hastily organised and the corpse taken for burial on the same day, at the village church, and the strange events continued as the funeral cortège was followed by a mysterious black boar to the graveyard. There, another violent storm began, with blazing flashes of lightning as the coffin was borne on to consecrated ground. So fierce was the tempest that the pallbearers abandoned the coffin and hid inside the parish church, whereupon the casket was lifted, in flames, by a whirlwind, which descended from the sinister leaden sky. This was to vanish seconds later out at sea in the wake once again of the black-sailed ship. The black boar also magically evaporated into thin air and was seen no more.

The strong similarities of this story to another famous tale about 'Cruel Coppinger' are uncanny. He was a Dane who arrived by ship at Morwenstow, in the north of the county, in the eighteenth century. Coppinger was supposed to have been endlessly pursued by revenue officers who wanted to put an end to his thriving smuggling and wrecking activities. In each story, the main character was an escapee from justice, utterly evil and on the wrong side of the law. They wrecked passing ships without remorse and often murdered the unfortunate victims who had escaped drowning.

Were there two separate 'beasts', or has legend here followed the style of the modern urban myth, where the same story appears over and over again in different places?

The Evidence

All the players in this stirring drama seem to have avoided inclusion into a modern world of local hauntings, and there have been no further sightings of the ghostly black-rigged ship at the Cape. However, as detailed in this book, several other spectral apparitions of phantom ships have been witnessed, up until the present day. These ghostly forms appear from dense mist, often with full sail, and glide silently through the water and sometimes inland, using valleys to move on to the headlands. The most famous ghost ship, at Porthcurno, bears striking similarities to the craft of this story.

DERELICT COTTAGE AT TREGESEAL: Was this the home of the evil wrecker?

The Location

The village of Tregeseal is easily visited from St Just. Leave the town by the A3071 towards St Ives. The road soon becomes the B3306. Turn right after a short distance, into the Nancherrow Valley. Head towards Tregeseal down a narrow road (SW375318).

Cape Cornwall and Priest's Cove (SW353318), where the wrecker was left by the rowing boat crew, is also reached from St Just, past the Cape Cornwall School. After approximately a mile, the narrow winding road passes the golf club and in a short distance reaches a car park, above Priest's Cove. This is an excellent area for walking, possessing beautiful open seascapes and dramatic cliff and beach scenery.

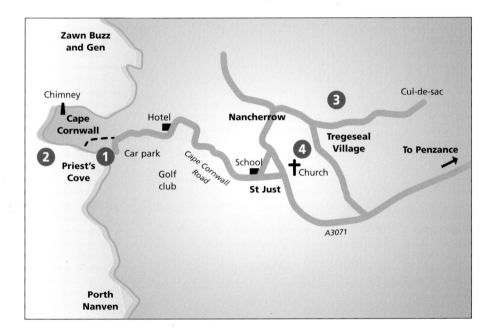

Map, reference to:

The Evil Wrecker of Tregeseal
1 The wrecker's landing point
2 The black ship's anchorage
3 The wrecker's cottage
4 The village church

Smugglers and Pirates

Abbey Street – Penzance
The Fair Trader of Mullion – Halzephron
Pengersick Castle – Praa Sands
The Smuggler's Screams – Hell's Mouth
The Pirate Ghosts – Penzance
The Legend of Penrose Manor – Sennen
The Admiral Benbow – Penzance
The First and Last Inn – Sennen

THE SMUGGLERS' GHOSTS

Oh dear, oh dear!
What is the world coming to, sure there's no smuggling now
and poor folk ha'n't got the means o' bettering 'emselves like proper Christians
Traditional Cornish Rhyme

Smugglers, or 'fair traders' as they preferred to be known, are certainly enshrined and interwoven into Cornish legend, history and folklore. They have been romanticised and demonised in almost equal proportions, and to some extent the truth is difficult to gauge. In reality it is likely that most smugglers of old were otherwise law-abiding, churchgoing citizens who took every opportunity to provide for their families. Sometimes this was the only way that they could survive the harsh Cornish life.

Unlike today's smugglers, who are in the main well-organised, professional groups, making vast sums of money, the traditional 'fair trader' was a more humble being. That said, smuggling tended to incorporate people from all walks of life and every part of the community. From farm-hand and fisherman to parson, gent and sometimes magistrate, all such persons were 'up for a bit o' fair trading'.

Them that ask no questions isn't told a lie;
Watch the wall my darlings while the gentlemen go by…

…immortalised in the Rudyard Kipling poem, was a typical Cornish saying about smugglers. One of the main reasons that relatively few people were prosecuted lay in the fact that so many people were involved, nobody would testify and everybody turned a blind eye. However, some smugglers were of a different breed, beyond the average everyday fellow making a quick sovereign. Sometimes they gained a fearsome reputation and their stories were catapulted through the mists of time, infamous 'celebrities', such as: Cruel Coppinger, the Black Prince; the Wrecker of Tregeseal; the Sennen wreckers; the fearsome brothers at Hell's Mouth; and perhaps the most infamous of them all, John Carter, the 'King of Prussia Cove', were names notable within this group.

Unfortunately, truth is not a major element of smuggling legend, despite stories about such activities being so widespread. Naturally, such fantastic tales included a number of ghostly stories about smugglers returning to seek vengeance or guard treasure. Perhaps this is somewhat ironic, because many smugglers were great tellers of ghost stories, often providing them as a means to keep prying eyes away from at their hidden locations. Also, smugglers were themselves fearful and full of respect for the supernatural. Spirits connected with the sea were to be taken seriously.

ABBEY STREET, PENZANCE

Abbey Street is situated very near Penzance's quay and was said to have been central for much of the activity in the area. There are many buildings here and in nearby New and Chapel streets which have links to the smuggling. Indeed, some of the vast network of tunnels used by the smugglers still exists underground to the present day (see The Admiral Benbow public house, p.50). Today Abbey Street includes Abbey Slip, which leads up to the

ABBEY STREET, PENZANCE: Several peculiar manifestations have been witnessed on the incline of this cobbled street which was once the main route through this historic town.

water's edge, adjacent to the dry dock. A modern swing-bridge means that ships can no longer moor up against the slip as they did over a century ago, when it would have been a very busy area. No doubt, when nightfall came, all sorts of strange characters could be seen here, engaged in their nocturnal activities, many illegal. Almost certainly, smugglers would be among them, carrying contraband to and from the ships docked here.

Abbey Street has several ghosts but the most common sightings seem to be linked to what may well be a group of smugglers. After nightfall, many people have witnessed a group of four men slowly making their way down the cobbled street, carrying what appears to be a crate or heavy box. They are described as wearing very old-fashioned clothes and sporting thick beards. Anyone unfortunate enough to encounter these strange fellows has soon discovered that as they approach they will suddenly vanish into thin air.

The Evidence

These strange ghosts (smugglers?) have been spotted on average three or four times a year, usually between 9 and 11pm. Several years ago, two young men were extremely shocked to encounter them. To their utter astonishment, when they spoke to the foursome, they disappeared, although previously they had seemed to be very solid.

Location

Drive into Penzance on the A30. Follow the road around to the left into Station Road (past the railway station). Stay in the left lane and drive along Wharf Road (car park to your left). Next turn right (just past the entrance on your left to the car park) just beyond the old lifeboat house. To the left is Abbey Street/Slip (SW476303). The sightings of the men are usually in the area between the top and middle of the incline, on the cobbled surface (map p.43).

THE FAIR TRADER OF MULLION

The phrase 'fair trader' was commonly used in Cornwall during the seventeenth and eighteenth centuries to describe someone who often was a very different type of person from the one implied by the term. 'Fair traders' were smugglers, raising their 'often large' profits by trading in stolen or pirated goods. Some items, such as wines, spirits or tobacco, were imported without customs duties being paid.

The risks of capture by the excise officers of the day were not as high as might be supposed since they were few in numbers and had an almost impossible task trying to patrol such extensive areas of coastline. Their objective was to prevent goods liable for excise duties from entering the country without payment of the taxes owed. However, since the smugglers tended to sell their wines and spirits more cheaply to the local population, it was unlikely that any of them would inform Customs and Excise about illicit trading. The smugglers' knowledge of their local coast, coves and hiding places also gave them a distinct advantage over the revenue men and government officials from London and the cities.

Although these 'fair traders' took a calculated gamble against discovery, the penalties if captured were horrific. Most of those convicted were hanged and then gibbeted in chains at the junction of some well-known local crossroads, in order to discourage other possible fair traders from the sheer folly of 'earning' this kind of 'easy money'. There were a number of notable locals connected with the smuggling trade, one being an eighteenth-century farmer and smuggler from Mullion, who had arranged a small shipload of full brandy and spirit casks to be delivered across Mount's Bay to Newlyn. He was delayed by business in nearby Helston and therefore set out towards Mullion late in the evening. Passing by the Halzephron cliff, between Berepper and Mullion, he was met by his ship's crew from their smuggling vessel. Halzephron cliff is situated in Gunwalloe parish and the men were some considerable distance from their locality. As they passed him, the farmer was struck by the realisation that they were all deathly silent and were dressed in torn and sodden clothing, and he took this as a clear sign that all his crew had been lost at sea that night.

On returning to his farm at Mullion, he learned that his boat had indeed sailed for Newlyn but after a sudden and violent storm in Mount's Bay, the heavily loaded vessel had sunk quickly, and all the crew had perished.

The Evidence

Such accounts regarding the return of the recent dead are common in many parts of the world and it would seem likely that those who have lost their lives unexpectedly and often violently, have returned briefly at death, to their loved ones. The sudden appearance and presence of the recent dead is seemingly to inform the close family, before the official news of death reaches them. Known as a 'crisis apparition', these phenomena are surprisingly frequent and can even involve the appearance of someone still alive, but in trauma.

There has been no recent ghostly re-enactment of the appearance of this particular crew from Mullion or of the fair trader. It must be assumed, therefore, that this was one of a growing catalogue of visitations after death to announce tragedy to friends or relatives.

Location

The Halzephron cliff (SW653213) is some distance from the main road, running from Helston to Lizard Point, and is accessed by a small and winding country lane, which eventually leads to Church Cove. From the Helston to Lizard road (A3083) take the narrow turning, signposted 'Berepper'. Near the pretty yet remote Halzephron Inn, one must park and join the south-west foot-path above Halzephron Cove and then proceed in a south-westerly direction for about half a mile to the headland.

It is worth noting that the recovered bodies of numerous shipwreck victims rest on the cliffs of the Cornish south-west peninsula in unmarked graves.

Below left: *HALZEPHRON CLIFF: This forebidding sheer promontory was the scene of the fair trader of Mullion's ghostly encounter.*

Below: *DOLLAR COVE, NEAR GUNWALLOE CHURCH: A popular beach in season, to the immediate north of Church Cove. There are known to be at least three shipwrecks off this promontory, one of which carries Spanish treasure, giving the cove its name.*

Like the 'phantom' crew at Halzephron cliff, these lie in different locations, such as Pistol Meadow, Grave's End, Porthleven and several other sites on the Lizard. The remoteness of the region, the number of corpses involved and the restrictions on the burial of unknown seafarers in hallowed ground, meant that these unconsecrated mass burials were not uncommon.

It is also well worth your time to continue along the road from the Halzephron Inn for the short distance to Church Cove. Here there is a squat but well-sheltered church just above the beach. Stories of Spanish treasure ships and wreckers still abound in this very attractive and typically Cornish beauty spot, where one can find constant Atlantic breakers, jagged cliffs and a deep sandy beach.

Below: *THE BELL TOWER, GUNWALLOE CHURCHYARD: This strangely separated bell tower gives rise to stories of hidden contraband and looted shipwreck merchandise.*

Below right: *GUNWALLOE CHURCH, AT CHURCH COVE: Scene of several ghostly incidents, overlooking the beautiful cove.*

In the summer, this location becomes very crowded, owing to the large National Trust car park some hundreds of yards short of the sands. There is an open tearoom in season but in winter, visitors must content themselves with simply enjoying the isolation of the bay and the ever-changing drama of the noisy Atlantic.

HALZEPHRON INN, NEAR BEREPPER VILLAGE: A very popular restaurant and hostelry, situated near Halzephron cliff.

Map, reference to:

The Fair Trader of Mullion (Halzephron cliff)

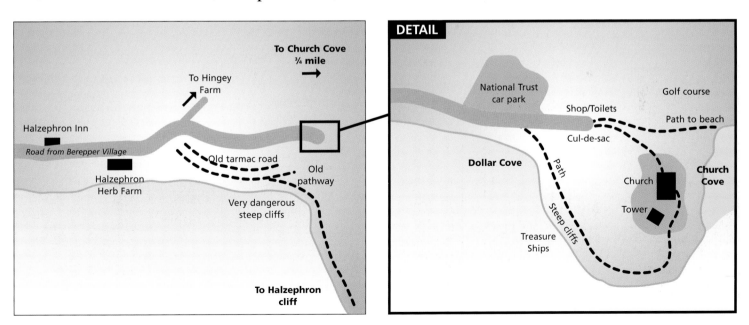

PENGERSICK CASTLE, PRAA SANDS

Pengersick Castle has a considerable number of ghosts and a widely acknowledged reputation for all things supernatural. One of its least-known spirits is believed to be that of a smuggler. During the seventeenth and eighteenth centuries, Pengersick Castle was left abandoned and in a poor state of repair. This, at a time of prevalent smuggling, must have been an open invitation, as it is suggested that the deserted interior was used for storing contraband. Indeed, several of the Pengersick legends and ghost stories seem to have appeared around this time to ward off the curious.

PENGERSICK CASTLE, PRAA SANDS: At present this is reputed to be the most active haunted location in the UK. Among its many ghosts is said to be a smuggler.

In addition, the infamous John Carter of nearby Prussia Cove is said to have owned a cottage just a stone's throw from Pengersick Castle. Today there is still said to be a large smugglers' tunnel leading underneath the castle and out towards Praa Sands beach. Who the spirit of the smuggler could be is not known, however, his presence has certainly been felt by several visitors, so perhaps he is still there trying to lay claim to a secret hoard.

On the subject of secret hoards, there are also rumours that the treasure of the Portuguese ship, the *St Anthony* wrecked at nearby Gunwalloe in 1526, was brought to Pengersick Castle and hidden in its walls. Some even claim the treasure is still there today, and that the ghosts of the crew and perhaps the thieves who took the wrecked cargo, may still haunt the castle looking for their riches.

The Evidence

Several visiting mediums have separately identified the presence of a smuggler within the last two or three years.

Unfortunately there are so many spirit presences at Pengersick that the smuggler has apparently taken something of a 'back seat'. His colleagues seem to have a more pressing mission to be noticed. Or perhaps the phantom smuggler is still trying to keep a low profile.

Location

Pengersick Castle (SW579283) is situated in Praa Sands. Take the A394 Penzance to Helston road and follow the signs to Pengersick/Praa Sands. The castle lies just before the holiday park on your right. Visits are by appointment only (at time of going to press the phone number is 01736 762579).

THE HAUNTED BEDROOM, PENGERSICK CASTLE: Focal point of the castle's supernatural manifestations. At night this room can take on a menacing character.

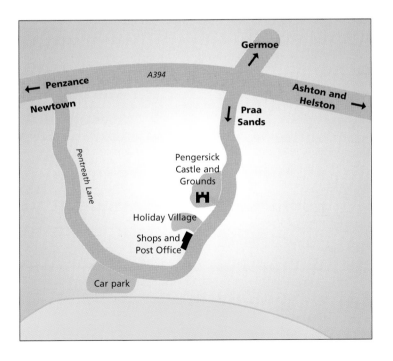

Map, reference to:

Pengersick Castle, Praa Sands

SCREAMS AT HELL'S MOUTH

The cliffs of Hell's Mouth are especially high and it is said that below the rocks is a vast network of tunnels and underground caves stretching for a great distance. For hundreds of years these passageways were used by smugglers, to store and hide their contraband. The particular band of fair traders who inhabited the area close to Hell's Mouth several centuries ago, were portrayed as a notoriously brutish group of men. Ever mindful that the penalty for their activities was death on the gallows, they would go to any lengths to avoid being captured or to have any of their ill-gotten gains confiscated.

Two of the gang, who were brothers, were particularly vicious creatures, known to all the locals by their bloodthirsty reputation, and matching each other in their ruthlessness. Finally, the authorities caught up with the group, after many years of tracking them, and several of the fellowship were taken into custody, among them the younger of the two brothers. All of them duly met their deaths, by execution at a public gathering. The remaining brother had somehow escaped capture and continued to commit crimes in the area, although now with an increased fervour. It seemed that he was trying to avenge his younger brother's punishment by causing as much mayhem as possible. It became a cat-and-mouse game as the authorities stepped up their attempts to bring him to justice, but finally, after several months, they did catch up with him. After a lengthy chase, the smuggler found that he was cornered at the cliffs of Hell's Mouth, with no means of escape.

There he stood high up on the dark brooding cliffs, with winds raging and the tempestuous grey sea rolling in, before a violent storm. His choice was simple: to allow himself to be captured and face the same fate as his brother, or turn and jump to certain death off the high cliff. Defiant to the end he gave one last shout, turned and leapt over the edge. The last thing that was heard was his bloodcurdling scream as he plummeted to the treacherous rocks beneath. Later his battered body was spotted far below, crumpled and lifeless, before the sea claimed it, thus cheating justice.

It is said that ever since, up on the lofty cliffs of Hell's Mouth, during dark and stormy weather with a howling wind, the cries and screams of the smuggler can still be heard, sending shocks of terror to anyone unfortunate enough to hear this deathly overture.

HELL'S MOUTH, NEAR GWITHIAN: This sheer 350-foot precipice is long associated with smuggling, shipwrecks, suicide and other macabre incidents.

The Evidence

Hundreds of people claim to hear screams in and around Hell's Mouth. However, in truth, it is difficult to believe they are not just hearing the howls of the wind, shrieks of a passing gull or a crying seal. The author has stood above it, gazing into the dark grey waters and imagined hearing deafening screams, just like a man shrieking in terror. Nevertheless, more evidence would be needed to believe it was supernatural and not just our ferocious elements. However, you never know!

Location

Hell's Mouth (SW603428) is about 1½ miles from Gwithian and approximately 3 miles from Portreath on the coast by the B3011. If venturing to these cliffs please do be careful, for the risks of falling over the unfenced 350-foot (approximately 100 metres) drop, during a strong gale are very pronounced, especially for the unwary.

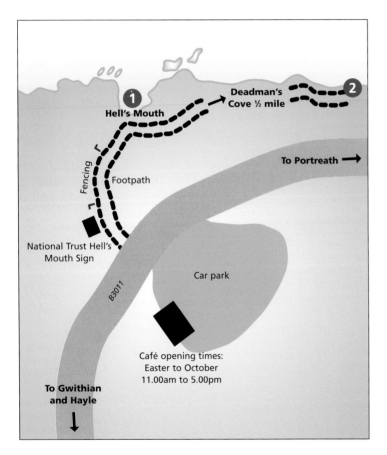

Hell's Mouth
Deadman's Cove ½ mile
Fencing
Footpath
To Portreath →
National Trust Hell's Mouth Sign
B3011
Car park
Café opening times:
Easter to October
11.00am to 5.00pm
To Gwithian and Hayle

Map, reference to:

Screams at Hell's Mouth, Deadman's Cove

1 Hell's Mouth cliffs (see p.36)
2 Deadman's Cove (see p.82)

THE REAL PIRATES OF PENZANCE

The operetta *Pirates of Penzance*, penned by Gilbert and Sullivan in 1879, has become a noted theatrical success, enjoyed by millions of people around the world. But who were these pirates? Well, in truth, there were no pirates *of* Penzance; the operetta is entirely fictional and there are no historical records about such a colourful band being based there. This is going to be a pretty short story, you may think! Many people, including locals, would be very surprised to learn that there is, however, a true story about pirates, associated with the town. It has all the classic elements of death, fear, tragedy and above all ghosts, to whet the appetite of any keen ghost hunter. In fact, the true story could well rival anything the literary or musical worlds can create.

Over the centuries, there have been countless dramas and disasters in Mount's Bay, within close proximity to the town of Penzance which, as a seafaring town since ancient times, has accumulated its fair share of ghostly and maritime tales. They run the gamut of shipwrecks, smuggling, battles, intrigue and untimely death. There are so many stories about the town and the bay that they would easily fill many volumes on their own. However, one event, occurring in 1760, has a very good chance of standing head and shoulders above all others.

On a particularly stormy day that year, a large Algerian corsair named the *Cavallo Bianco* (White Horse) got into terrible difficulties out in Mount's Bay in the early hours of the morning. After a ferocious battle against the elements, the ship was finally thrown up on the Chimney Rocks, just off Penzance. (Chimney Rocks jut out from the right of Penzance's bathing pool, in front of the promenade.) The ship was so badly damaged that it began to sink and the crew, realising their predicament, began to jump from the wrecked ship into the cold, dark waters.

Fortunately, the beach was only a short distance away and so the majority of the crew succeeded in reaching the shore. The bedraggled party of well over

CHIMNEY ROCKS, PENZANCE: Here the Cavallo Bianco *and its crew met their fate, and the ghostly pirates are said to walk. The photograph was taken at very low spring tides. The imposing rocky fortress of St Michael's Mount can be seen in the left background.*

a hundred men was soon heading up the beach, known as the Western Green. Several local people had gathered in the area, either to offer assistance or to stare at the spectacle unfolding before them. But soon all thoughts of assistance were put to one side as the realisation spread amongst the group that this was no ordinary band of men. The mariners were a strange bunch, wearing peculiar clothes. They were dark skinned, with turbans and carrying scimitars. Indeed, it did not take people long to realise that this was a pirate crew from North Africa. At this time such men had a fearsome reputation and many of the locals immediately fled for their lives.

A similar incident had long existed in the annals of Penzance. Just over a hundred years before a pirate vessel had entered the harbour at night and its occupants had kidnapped many residents – men, women and children. They were never seen again. Not surprising then that most of these onlookers did not wish to find out what the crew's intentions were. Nevertheless, a group of men was hurriedly assembled, a volunteer band that had been gathered and armed in case of trouble with France or other possible foreign invaders. Now they collected their weapons and headed towards the beach.

Nobody was sure what would happen next, but they need not have worried. The pirates, shocked and exhausted by their efforts, were not ready to put up much resistance. They were soon rounded up and taken to a local building, the 'Folly House' (situated near to the present-day amusement arcade). There the men were kept imprisoned in strict quarantine over several weeks for fear of disease, though it was said that they were looked after well. Indeed they became quite a local curiosity, with many people coming to take a look at the strangers. Eventually, they were transported to Falmouth and more of the story can be found in local history books.

However, to return to the night of the shipwreck… soon a grim discovery was made on the beach. It seemed that some of the pirate crew had been much less fortunate, as over the coming hours 14 battered bodies were thrown up on to the sands and left scattered across the beach. Swiftly the authorities dealt with the 'problems' by burying the men where they lay, deep under the sands and in keeping with the custom of the time. They received no formal or religious ceremony and were simply interred in a manner which caused much consternation amongst their fellow shipmates.

This is an incredible story, but nevertheless true and well documented in history books. Many people have concerned themselves as to the fate of the bodies, with the truth being that nobody knows. It is likely that with the passage of time and the shifting of sands, their skeletons have long disintegrated or may just lie somewhere under the present-day road or promenade.

Often it is claimed that people who fail to receive a proper burial may become lost souls, remaining earthbound until the act of disrespect is corrected. So a story such as this should surely be a prerequisite for supernatural shenanigans, and, as if not to disappoint, there does seem to be a ghost story linked to these events. There are several people who have been in this area in the small hours of the morning and claim to have witnessed a bizarre spectacle.

They have described a large group of men, presumably 14, wearing strange clothes, sporting turbans and looking extremely wet and bedraggled, as they slowly head up the shingle beach towards the promenade. Most of the witnesses have immediately felt a sensation of dread and realised they have had an encounter with the 'other side', so nobody has stayed around long enough to find out where the men are heading. It would be an unbelievable coincidence if what such people claim to have seen bears no relationship to this fascinating story. The apparitions may well be the lost souls of these pirates, restless spirits, fated to remain at the scene of their demise.

It seems that these figures are most likely to appear on dark and stormy nights when the tide is out. They walk very steadily across the shingle, with an almost pleading expression etched on their damp faces. Perhaps they will remain as desperate ghouls until they each receive their rightful burials.

The Evidence

There has been at least one known sighting within the last few years, although there were no additional supporting witnesses. The authors are not aware of any other recent sightings. Certainly though, others have been recorded within living memory, including one in 1943, and another in 1958. Several other strange occurrences have been experienced on this same beach, which may be linked to the ghosts.

One man insisted that he saw the figures about eight years ago whilst beach fishing. This spectacle occurred at about 3am and he was so terrified that he ran from the beach, leaving his fishing equipment behind. In 1999 a renowned medium assured the author that she had sensed a large number of lost spirits in the area, who refused to 'step into the light' as they declined to accept that this is their next step. She believes that they remain earthbound until they can settle their earthly ties. Perhaps a religious service or proper burial is the only thing to set the souls to rest. Therefore you may wish to dust off that bucket and spade and act as the Good Samaritan!

Location

Drive into Penzance on the A30 past the railway station and take the left lane into Wharf Road. Continue past the harbour and the Dolphin Tavern; on your left is the promenade (SW474298). After the famous open-air bathing pool, walk on to the promenade and look down. You may see a small shingle beach and possibly make out some of the Chimney Rocks (SW476297), breaking the surface of the sea depending on the state of the tide. (If you are planning to visit during stormy weather, please be careful of the sweeping waves; the authors don't want you starring in their next book about ghosts!)

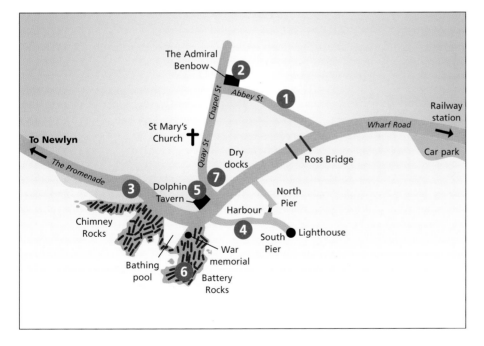

Map, reference to:

1 Abbey Street, Penzance (see p.27)
2 Spirits at the Inn, The Admiral Benbow (see p.50)
3 The Real Pirates of Penzance (see p.39)
4 The Black Dog of Penzance Harbour (see p.58)
5 Spirits at the Inn, The Dolphin Tavern (see p.91)
6 Screams at the Battery Rocks (see p.125)
7 The Sailor's Ghost, Penzance (see p.87)

The authors run Ghost Walks from the Railway Station area around Penzance throughout the year on special nights weekly. More information from Tourist Information Centres locally.

THE LEGEND OF PENROSE MANOR

This simple Cornish farmhouse, seemingly of Georgian origin from first appearances, is situated at the end of a private track leading in the direction of Land's End, at the southern edge of Sennen village and off the A30. It is a dwelling full of interest and surprises, though access is limited as it is a privately owned farm. The author paid a rewarding visit some eighteen years ago and can remember the long approach down a rough stony track in his companion's car, and the sudden descent across a nearly dry stream bed before the sharp, uphill climb to the dwelling with its cluster of granite outbuildings. The main farm was of a longhouse design, fronted by granite walls and lawns; an intriguing place.

Our tale of Penrose Manor begins in the late-seventeenth century, with the ancient Cornish family of Penrose for whom the house was named. Even today the place exudes an atmosphere of remoteness from its surrounds, so 350 years ago this farm and its land must have seemed totally detached from existing civilisation, standing on this isolated peninsula jutting out into the Atlantic Ocean.

'Survival of the fittest' was certainly the philosophy of those times and the head of the Penrose family, Ralph, lived as a smuggler, working with his cousin William. Both men sailed in their locally built craft and were noted for helping the less fortunate of the parish. They traded illegally with France for wines, spirits, provisions and tobacco, most of which involved the evasion of customs duty payments.

On the untimely death of his wife, Ralph, a heartbroken man, spent longer periods of time at sea, with his son (who was only seven years of age) amongst the crew. John Penrose, Ralph's younger brother, managed Penrose Manor in Ralph's absence and the successful 'free trade' with France made the family into a local legend.

One cold winter's evening, Ralph's laden vessel was wrecked during a storm on the dreaded Cowloe Reef (SW348267), off Sennen Cove. Ralph, William and the young boy were all presumed to have perished along with the ship's crew in the stormy waters. Brother John Penrose had been summoned to Sennen Beach and with some servants was urged to organise a rescue attempt for the stricken crew. But he refused to act and left them to drown in the icy sea. It later transpired that the young Penrose boy, now heir to Penrose Manor, had in fact miraculously survived the ferocious storm.

From that moment on, John Penrose began a regime of organised terror, piracy, violence and increasing lawlessness in the locality and no one dared to resist him. His merciless band of cronies enjoyed long nights of debauchery and drinking at the manor, and their crimes went unpunished. During one winter's snowstorm, wolves were sighted on top of Sennen's cliffs and so began a drunken hunt by the renegade band, leaving behind John Penrose and his best friend, the captain of the pirate ship, to indulge heavily in copious quantities of liquor at the manor. The crew returned much later, only to discover that no trace of the young nephew could be found at the house. Even as servants spent several days searching for the child, John coldly announced that the boy had certainly perished during the hunt, perhaps by falling over a cliff.

Subsequently John's reckless pattern of living reached even greater extremes. He gambled away much of the estates and supported the reign of terror, rape and pillage over the local surrounding area. The captain of John's pirate ship soon left his employ without explanation and vanished to Devon. The next winter, between Christmas and New Year, at one of John's drunken parties, a stranger came to the manor to seek shelter and food. The guest was given Ralph's old bedroom and before falling asleep, he parted the curtains to view the disgraceful revelry below in the courtyard.

Suddenly, the scene was enveloped in a swirling, dense fog, followed by the loud roaring of the sea, which was over 1½ miles away. The noise intensified and soon a phantom ship was seen riding spectral waves into the courtyard. A chilling re-enactment followed, apparently the events of Ralph's shipwreck years earlier. The latter's face appeared to scream up at the watching stranger, urging, 'William Penrose, avenge the murder of your cousin's young son.'

The guest at the manor later proved to be William Penrose, who had by some miracle escaped death during the shipwreck. Unbeknown to all, he had gone abroad and lived in hiding. In fitful sleep that night, William was visited by the ghost of his cousin's young son and was told that the captain of the pirate ship had murdered him on John's instructions. The body lay in the orchard in a shallow grave, and the ghost requested the exhumation of his body from its wretched resting place, so that he could be buried in the consecrated ground of Sennen churchyard (SW357256). Only in this manner, could the ghost find peace at last.

SENNEN CHURCHYARD: Possible site of the rein-terred body of Ralph Penrose's thirteen-year-old son. The damaged inscription reads '…aged 13 years…'.

William Penrose revealed his identity next morning to the head servant and then left the manor for Plymouth, in order to seek out the murderous captain. William found him dying in a poorhouse in the city's docklands and the captain confessed to the heinous crime; a murder on John's instruction.

William thus returned to Penrose Farm, and with the help of the head servant, started to dig in the orchard where, as instructed, he found the piteous remains of the young lad. As requested, he interred the body in the church-yard. Returning to the manor house, the two men found John Penrose hanging from a beam in the bedroom once used by his brother Ralph.

Later William left the family house because he claimed it to be haunted, and departed for Palestine. He sold the estate to another local smuggler, who restored the building, with some alterations, to a large farmhouse.

Thus the story concludes, but what about the authenticity of the ghost?

PENROSE MANOR, NEAR SENNEN: Home of the infamous Penrose smugglers and the site of the phantom ship and murder of Ralph's young son. Note the courtyard wall in the left middle ground, enclosing the 'haunted courtyard' out of sight behind it.

The Evidence

During past centuries, there were regular reports of ghostly activities in and around Penrose Manor. In 1981 a friend of the author's, who knew the resident family, gained permission for a visit and the use of metal detectors around the lawns and courtyard to search for the supposed buried treasure of John Penrose.

Perhaps unsurprisingly, no treasure was found but some very interesting items were recovered, including the head of a silver riding-crop, from the nearby stream and a silver, eighteenth-century Penrose-crested knife and spoon, recovered from beneath the front lawn of the farmhouse. These items must have lain there, undisturbed, for over 250 years, perhaps dropped by servants after an outside picnic. Four months later, on another 'detecting' mission, the matching silver crested fork also turned up, delighting the family.

The tour of the manor house provided fresh evidence of haunted activity. The family's two young children both related how they often heard footsteps on the staircase, heading from the 'hanging room'. They also claimed that on several occasions each year they had witnessed a ghost on the stairs, which was believed to be that of John Penrose.

The bedroom of Ralph Penrose was palpably cold, damp and eerie, whilst the beam from which his brother John hanged was still there. The atmosphere of that room was so dank and oppressive that it certainly fitted the requirements of the legend. The house itself was a remarkable place. For instance, imagine the author's surprise in finding an exquisite Tudor fireplace in the oldest part of the building, for this alone would re-date the building to far earlier than its Georgian exterior would suggest.

PENROSE MANOR ENTRANCE: The entrance to the long, narrow and winding approach to this famous manor house.

As for the courtyard shipwreck story… There is claimed to be a phantom ship, reported on occasions, floating up Penberth Valley from the Atlantic, towards Penrose Manor and out on to the valley head. The evidence available seems to bear out much of this fantastic story and Penrose Manor is still almost certainly a very haunted building, centuries after the terrifying sequence of events ceased.

Location

Penrose Manor (SW378256) is private property and, as such, access is only with the owner's permission. Please remember, trespass is an offence, so do not ignore correct procedure. The manor access road is reached from the A30 in Sennen village by taking the first left before the right turn to Sennen Cove, when moving in the direction of Land's End. Follow this winding lane through Trevear Farm and then continue along the narrow road for about a mile to where the Penrose track leaves the lane by a right turning, marked 'Penrose'. The narrow stream and ford (now dry) lie about half a mile ahead of you. There is also a path leading from the A30, through Trevorian Farm and Trevear Farm, to Penrose Farm.

The orchard where the nephew child was buried has mostly disappeared but a solitary tree is said to mark the grave. It stands alone, close to the manor, in the surrounding meadowland. During a gloriously red summer sunset, the tree casts long shadows over the grass, appearing dark and menacing, when silhouetted against the skyline.

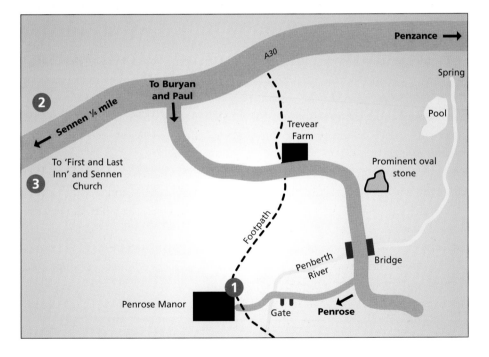

Map, reference to:

1 The Legend of Penrose Manor (see p.44)
2 The Hooper, Sennen Cove (see p.122)
3 Spirits at the Inn, 'The First and Last' (see p.51)

ADMIRAL BENBOW PUBLIC HOUSE, PENZANCE: This much photographed and visited hostelry is reputed to have been the scene of several apparitions, in particular what are believed to be smugglers and a distraught young lady, pining for her lost love.

SPIRITS AT THE INN – THE ADMIRAL BENBOW, PENZANCE

The Admiral Benbow dates back to at least the seventeenth century, and is notorious for the smuggling activity which centred on the building in bygone days. There is still a figure on the roof of the inn today, set in place to portray this smuggling heritage, said to represent Octavius Lanyon, leader of the smugglers' band of men. Contraband was brought through a series of tunnels, networked underneath this and other buildings. Some of the passageways remain today and although they are not open to the public, many people who have been in them claim to have heard mysterious footsteps approaching. At least one reliable witness has also claimed to see a ghostly figure in the dark recess. Perhaps Octavius and his fellow fair traders remain here today in a less human form.

The pub is also believed to be haunted by a young lady named Annabelle, who in the eighteenth century died of a broken heart when her lover was lost at sea. Many people claim to sense her presence in the cellars and she is also seen gazing from an upstairs window. In particular, male members of staff often experience a strange 'tap on the shoulder', when no real person is anywhere near.

The Evidence

A great number of people have claimed to hear the footsteps in the tunnels in recent years. Annabelle's presence is frequently felt. The author also knows of reliable friends and relations who have experienced these phenomena without any prior knowledge of the haunting.

Location

The Admiral Benbow lies at the crossroads of Chapel Street and Abbey Street (SW475302). Follow the directions for Abbey Street (map p.43) and walk or drive to the top. The Admiral Benbow is the distinctive white building on the corner. Of particular note is the aforementioned figure of a smuggler lying prone on the roof, reputed to be the infamous Octavius Lanyon, engaged in resisting a raid by Customs and Excise officers. The building's interior houses an outstanding collection of maritime and diving memorabilia associated with the late treasure hunter Roland Morris. The inn itself, at the time of writing, also serves an excellent array of seafood and other dishes.

SPIRITS AT THE INN – THE FIRST AND LAST, SENNEN

As the name indicates, you can travel little further by land than to this location; Land's End lies just slightly further on. This famous inn is almost certainly haunted, which seems to be common knowledge in the vicinity. The most likely 'candidate' seems to be a woman called Annie Treeve who presided over the inn in the early part of the nineteenth century and was a formidable character. She also ran the smuggling and wrecking operations in the area. Ultimately, Customs and Excise caught up with the group and Annie turned King's Evidence to save her own skin.

For her perceived 'treason', the locals enacted their utmost revenge. Annie was seized and taken to Sennen Beach, where she was staked out and left to drown with the incoming tide. After her demise, she was taken back to the inn and laid out in an upstairs room before burial in an unmarked grave.

Perhaps not surprisingly, her ghost is said to have been extremely restless ever since. Perhaps she aims to seek vengeance on her killers and simply cannot accept that her smuggling days are over.

The Evidence

There have been many reported paranormal happenings over a long period and, without doubt, this is still an active haunting. The author had the good fortune to carry out an investigation at the property and can conclude that

FIRST AND LAST INN, SENNEN: Home of Annie Treeve, smuggler, whose eerie presence still fills the building.

many things happened without rational explanation. Unfortunately, owing to confidentiality, the details cannot be published.

Location

Drive on the A30 towards Land's End. As you enter Sennen village you will see the church and churchyard to your left. Prepare to take the next turning to the left, which leads to the inn's private car park. The inn (SW357255) can be seen from the road and is an attractive building, constructed in 1620 and steeped in legend. Inside you will find a plaque about Annie Treeve and below this is 'Annie's Well', covered by toughened glass, a deep shaft which was revealed several years ago when the floor collapsed inside the inn. It is now lit from inside to allow customers to look down into it, and seems the perfect hiding place for smuggled contraband.

If you walk into Sennen churchyard, next to the inn, spend a few minutes looking for the possible grave location of the young murdered son of Ralph Penrose. You may even find the gravestone which the authors thought most likely to be his, inscribed: '…aged 13 years' (maps p.63 and p.124).

Animal Ghosts

The Cliff Creature – Carbis Bay
The Phantom White Horse – St Ives
The Black Dog – Penzance
The Daisy Dog – Nanjizal Bay

THE CLIFF CREATURE, CARBIS BAY

Here is a bizarre tale from the splendid holiday village of Carbis Bay, near St Ives, about a peculiar creature believed to haunt a cliff path. Said to be only vaguely human in appearance, it is described as being quite tall and having a gigantic, faceless head in the shape of a large pumpkin. The figure is said to move in a peculiar jerky manner and to walk with an unnatural sway as it moves swiftly along the cliff path, before suddenly vanishing over the edge as if about to plummet towards the sea below. Anyone brave enough to look down from the cliff top has been unable to see any trace of the strange manifestation. Nobody has any idea as to what the strange beast might be but undoubtedly it has left several people in a state of shock and terror after an encounter.

The Evidence

Some examples of chance meetings with this creature are described by Michael Williams in his book *Supernatural in Cornwall*, although there are few recent instances. Nonetheless, there were said to be several in the 1960s. One report described the figure as a 'thing without a face, jogging alongside,

THE HAUNTED CLIFF PATH, CARBIS BAY: This almost forgotten, overgrown track overlooks the cliffs at Carbis Bay. It is alleged to be the home of a terrifying creature.

Map, reference to:

The Cliff Creature, Carbis Bay

wearing grey robes and solid; there was no shadow and then it simply vanished'. Another person saw the creature scratching at the floor before it jumped up like an ape and jumped off the cliff.

Location

Drive into Carbis Bay on the A3074 to St Ives road. At the signpost indicating a left turn to 'Trencrom', turn right into Portheptra Road (marked for railway station). Go past the church on the left and near the end of the road turn right into Headland Road. Park at the end and look for the green sign to the footpath and walk left towards the cliff path (SW535386). Continue back along the path in the direction of Carbis Bay, towards the cliff of Carrack Gladden and Porth Kidney Sands. Most sightings have occurred along this quarter-mile stretch of overgrown path.

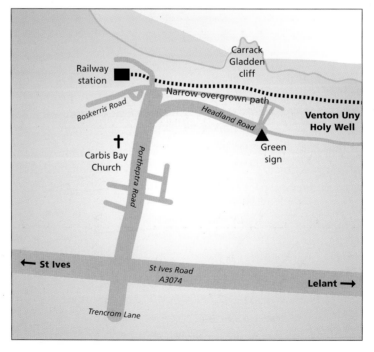

THE PHANTOM WHITE HORSE OF ST IVES

Porthgwidden Beach at St Ives has a well-known story about a beautiful white horse which is said to haunt this particular stretch of sand. Sometime in the nineteenth century the horse and its rider were often seen riding along the beach at Porthgwidden, where the man would dismount and go for a swim.

One evening, the pair came to the beach and, as usual, the man jumped down from his horse and waded into the sea. This time, however, disaster struck as the man was swept out by the rising swell and was drowned. His trusty white horse was later found wandering the beach alone.

Despite such a passage of time, it is said that the horse still returns to the beach to wait for his beloved master. In the past he has often been seen galloping along Island Road, before moving on to the beach itself. On other occasions, it is claimed, the horse has also been sighted returning from the beach with a figure on his back, undoubtedly the hapless owner.

The Evidence

During the nineteenth century this haunting was apparently a frequent occurrence, in the proximity of Porthgwidden Beach. There are far fewer recent sightings but, perhaps more interestingly, there have been several audio experiences which may well relate to the horse. Numerous people claim to have heard the very clear sound of horse's hoof-beats moving towards the beach.

For example, in 2001 a family was staying in a nearby holiday cottage. It was after midnight when they all detected a sound of a horse trotting past their residence. The whole family debated the experience the next morning, because they could not understand why a

PORTHGWIDDEN BEACH, ST IVES: This popular tourist beach was photographed in mid-July. As darkness falls it takes on a more sinister countenance and at times it is said that a phantom white horse returns here.

ISLAND ROAD, ST IVES: A narrow ancient route leading to the Island. This is where the phantom white horse is often heard trotting, during the hours of darkness.

horse should be in this area, especially at such a late hour. Unfortunately, none of them had looked out of the window, although later that day they were shocked to hear the story of the Porthgwidden horse during a St Ives ghost walk, and wondered if they had indeed heard this supernatural creature. It is also worth mentioning that on many occasions, those staying in the proximity of Island Road have testified to clearly hearing horse's hoof-beats at night, although they had no prior knowledge of this local folk-tale.

On 27 February 2002, a woman visiting St Ives made an early-morning visit to nearby Porthmeor Beach. No one else was around but suddenly, from nowhere appeared a white horse in the distance, galloping towards her. She found it odd for a rider to be out so early, particularly in the middle of the town of St Ives. She glanced down for a moment and on looking back was surprised to find that the horse and rider had vanished. She could not under-stand where they had gone but finally decided there must be a rational explanation, before continuing to enjoy her solitude. Later in the year, to her consternation, she learned for the first time about the story of the phantom white horse. Had the white horse made an impromptu appearance on Porthmeor Beach, thus adding a possible new sighting in addition to the more numerous audio re-enactments?

Location

Follow the same directions as for the 'Lady and the Lantern' story. From the car park, turn right and walk down past the café to your left and straight on to Porthgwidden Beach (SW523412). Ghostly happenings apart, it is an ideal place for enjoying sunbathing or other beach activities, though can be crowded at certain times. During the summer, seals often venture on to the sands, so please respect the animals' right to privacy.

You may also find some beautiful artistic sand creations on Porthgwidden Beach. Over several years an artist has been sculpting some incredible sand replicas on the beach, of a horse or horses. To see these is well worth a visit in itself and they are, in the author's opinion, the work of genius far surpassing much of the 'official' art to be found in the numerous galleries of St Ives town.

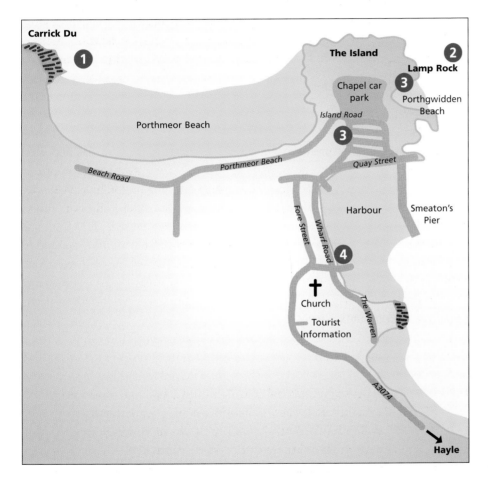

Map, reference to:

St Ives

1 The Boatman of Porthmeor Beach (see p.93)
2 The Lady and the Lantern (see p.95)
3 The Phantom White Horse (see p.55)
4 *The Sally* (see p.15)

The authors run Ghost Walks from Street-an-Pol regularly throughout the year. More information from Tourist Information Centres locally.

THE BLACK DOG OF PENZANCE HARBOUR

Almost every area around the country has a tale to tell about a strange black dog, which is said to be a harbinger of doom for the unfortunate witness, bringing at best bad luck, at worst, death. For example, there is 'Black Shuck' in East Anglia, 'Old Trash' on Merseyside, the 'Gwyllgi' in Wales, 'Shriker' in Lancashire, the 'Moddey Doo' on the Isle of Man, and many more besides.

The enduring common theme is for those who spot such a strange creature to fall ill, with death following as a matter of course. This occurs frequently within a short space of time; a few days, or sometimes just minutes later. The poor souls who have come across these 'hell-hounds' are ill-starred indeed.

For some strange and unknown reason the harbour area of Penzance seems to have its own black dog, said to be about the size of a small Labrador, which has often been seen and later linked to several ill-fated events. This creature does not seem to be in any way as ferocious as some of its more famous counterparts but, nevertheless, it would appear to be acting as a herald of catastrophe.

There have been many stories linked to the hound, some of which are related here. Many following the same theme have come from sailors frequenting the harbour, who have told of an apparently friendly dog which would be seen around the area for a short period of time before taking its leave. Eerily, the dog would be seen only by certain individuals, whose companions seemed unable to see it. More disturbingly, though, those who were befriended by the animal would invariably be struck down before long by serious illness and, in due course, death, or it seemed were fated to die in tragic circumstances some time later.

One such tale was of a sailor from a French ship, many years ago, who had spoken to his crewmates about a small black dog which had been pestering him. This creature had even tried to get on to the boat itself. However, none of his friends seemed able to see the hound themselves because every time they looked for it, it had gone. Strangely enough, the same evening after this had happened, the sailor suddenly became unwell. He was usually a perfectly healthy man yet within a few hours his condition had deteriorated so much that he had to be rushed to hospital. His fellow sailors were devastated to hear later that night that their friend was dead.

SOUTH PIER, PENZANCE HARBOUR: Said by locals to be the site for numerous visitations by a ghostly black dog, a harbinger of doom.

In a more recent tale from only thirty to forty years ago, a small fishing boat was moored in the harbour overnight. The crew decided to go for a few drinks in the Dolphin Tavern (opposite the harbour) where they enjoyed a happy few hours carousing.

One of the crew had to leave his companions early, having been deputed to go back and check on the boat. When his shipmates returned to the vessel, the man told them that he had been kept company by a friendly little black dog, which had come aboard just after he had arrived back onboard. It had stayed with him for the whole evening, yet strangely, moments before the other men returned, this dog had suddenly disappeared, without warning.

The next day the boat set off from the harbour to do some fishing out in Mount's Bay, only to be caught up in a ferocious and unexpected storm. For a long time the crew struggled to regain control of their boat, until finally the strong winds eased and everything became calm. It was then that the shout went up from one of the crew, 'Man overboard!' One of the crew was missing; indeed it was the man who had reported seeing the black dog. He was never seen again, at least not alive, and so it would seem that he had become another victim of the dog.

The Evidence

Whether or not the creature serves as a warning for unsuspecting witnesses is unclear, but certainly there have been many other cases of people seeing the strange animal, including some quite recent reports. It would seem to be a good idea to be wary of any unusually friendly stray black dogs which one might come across in the harbour area of Penzance.

Location

The harbour can be found following the directions for Battery Rocks. The most common area for sightings of the black dog seems to be the South Pier (SW477299). If you feel sufficiently sceptical about the dangers, or at least exercising due caution (!), walk down to the right of the Meadery Restaurant and opposite the Dolphin Tavern. At the end of the pier is a lighthouse and a small bridge crossing to the other pier. This is also the departure point for the *Scillonian* ferry to the beautiful Isles of Scilly where you will find many large ships moored including, on occasions, naval vessels and tall ships. It is well worth a stroll around, particularly if you are interested in shipping and maritime fare (map p.43).

THE DAISY DOG

This unusual tale, originating from sixteenth-century China, intriguingly involves an oriental princess, a gift of priceless Pekinese dogs, and their tragic demise off the Cornish coast. In those days only the Imperial family were permitted to own the Pekinese breed, and when England's Queen Elizabeth I was crowned in 1559, the emperor decided that the dogs would make a fitting royal gift. His daughter, the Imperial princess, was appointed to be their escort on the long and dangerous journey to England, travelling over land and sea.

The Pekinese bitch would sleep in a carved ivory box for safety when travelling, whilst the male dog ran free in the wagon or ship. After three months the bitch gave birth to five puppies and nestled in her ivory home, whilst the little dog guarded the royal princess and his own canine family. On reaching France, a Cornish sailing vessel was chartered to convey the princess and her gift up the Channel to London. The crew, however, deeply feared the foreign lady with her ivory box and slanting eyes, believing that she must be carrying priceless treasure in the chest, whilst, to them, her eyes indicated that she must be a demon.

As the ship moved into the approaches to the English Channel, it faced a terrible and sudden storm off Land's End. The crew, blaming their foreign 'demon' passenger and her cargo for their plight, threw her and the chest overboard into the violent waves. One of the crew was severely bitten on his hand by the little dog, as he heaved the box and its contents over the ship's rail.

In a short time the storm cleared, the wind veered round and the vessel safely entered Mount's Bay (the large stretch of water from Mousehole to Lizard Point where shelter for sailing ships could be gained, depending on the wind direction.) By daybreak, the body of the Chinese princess and her ivory box were washed ashore on Nanjizal or Mill Bay, a few miles east of Land's End. And so began the 'Daisy Dog' haunting.

Later that day, a local farmer discovered the girl's body and the box with its pathetic contents. Only the little Pekinese dog was still alive, although it was undoubtedly dying. It watched the Cornishman dig a grave under the cliffs, placing all the bodies together in the sand.

At this point, the reader should note that such a burial, in unconsecrated ground, was common until the mid-nineteenth century, since only affirmed Christian sailors could be buried in local churchyards after a shipwreck. Foreigners and unknown mariners did not meet the criteria. As such, many Cornish beaches and cliff tops contain the sad remains of victims lost at sea.

The grave being completed, the farmer gathered a large bunch of wild daisies from the cliff top and placed them on the burial mound, in the shape of a cross. The little dog, now almost dead, was placed among the daisies and with a last gesture of gratitude, licked the farmer's hand and passed away.

Meanwhile, the French ship, from which the princess had been thrown, reached the safe harbour of Newlyn with news of the storm, the Chinese 'demon' and her treasure chest. The bitten sailor died in agony a few days later and so the story began that he had been cursed by the bite of the dog. Before long, news about the exact location of the grave and its contents reached port and tales soon arose, claiming that a ghostly dog was supposedly guarding the burial site. Should it bite you, it was said to herald certain death.

The Evidence

Over the past centuries, several people who have walked across the sands at Nanjizal Bay, reputedly have been bitten by the Daisy Dog. In particular this seems to happen to those caught deliberately disturbing the sand's surface. As recently as the nineteenth century, a youth was said to have found a fragment of carved ivory at the base of the cliffs. On picking up this object he felt a savage bite to the hand and, despite having suffered only minor injuries, died a short time later. It would appear that his actions had offended the ghostly dog. As far as the authors are aware, no recent reports of further victims of the phantom dog have materialised, but who can be sure this means that he lies dormant?

Location

Nanjizal Bay is located at grid reference SW355237. Having taken the A30 to Land's End car park, walk towards the cliffs to the east of the hotel and join the path, travelling in a south-easterly direction away from the hotel. Nanjizal Bay can only be reached today on foot, as road access is private. The walk takes about three-quarters of an hour along the top of precipitous cliffs, with a drop of hundreds of feet. Children and pets are not recommended to venture without strict supervision. People do fall over cliffs all too often in Cornwall, particularly in the summer, so please take extra care if you choose to take this route.

The area also has the additional hazard of Britain's only poisonous snake, the adder. Although these are now rare, do be vigilant. Walkers and dogs must take note of the narrow paths where occasionally an adder may still be found basking in the sun. Whilst the walk up to the bay is truly outstanding in its sheer picturesque beauty, especially on a warm summer's day, digging in the sandy beach on arrival is not recommended, unless you have a strong nerve or a resolute denial of superstition and the supernatural.

Of further interest, it should be noted that the visible remains of the shipwreck, SS *Cardiff*, can be seen at certain

Map, reference to:

1 SS *Cardiff* wreck (Daisy Dog) (see p.61)
2 The Daisy Dog (see p.61)
3 The Spirits at the Inn, First and Last, Sennen (see p.51)
4 The Irish Lady Rock (see p.98)

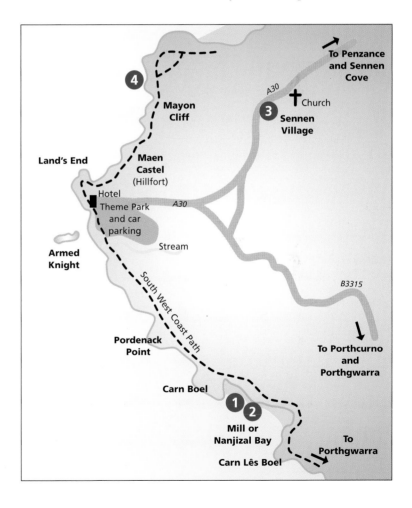

low tides near to the cliffs at the western edge of Nanjizal. Her seaweed-encrusted boilers have lain there since 1899 as a further tragic dimension to this remote and spooky location.

PRINT OF SS LLANDAFF, NANJIZAL BAY: A small Cardiff collier ship stranded at the western end of the bay, near Land's End. The seaweed-covered boilers of the SS Cardiff, another shipwreck, can be seen at very low tides close to this stack (right).

Sailors' Spirits

The Cottage Ghost – Newlyn
The Sweethearts – Porthgwarra
Pistol Meadow – Lizard Point
The Seamen's Morgue – Portreath
The Black Figure – Deadman's Cove
The Seamen's Ghost – Zennor
The Sailor's Ghost – Penzance
The Dolphin Tavern – Penzance
The Boatmen of Porthmeor Beach – St Ives

THE NEWLYN COTTAGE GHOST

For this story we must travel to the picturesque fishing village of Newlyn, near Penzance. With its old harbour wall, still standing but surrounded by large new quays, the small port is rapidly expanding into the twenty-first century. The new fish market provides catches for the local area, as well as London and the Continent, and things look promising for Newlyn's future, as long as the fishing industry remains strong.

Newlyn, as an old port, has retained many of the narrow granite-walled lanes and closely linked cottages. A slow ramble through the back streets evokes the Victorian world of yesteryear. It was here that the authors found a cottage with a particularly compelling story.

In 1999 a young couple living in the property experienced a frightening paranormal incident. Late one evening, whilst they were relaxing in front of their television, they were startled by an unusual noise, immediately followed by the appearance of a burly fisherman, standing in their cottage, beside the front door. The young husband challenged the intruder, who failed to speak. As a result he charged at the fisherman to intercept him.

The stranger appeared to be a solid human being but as the young man lunged at him, he was staggered to find that he passed right through the figure and ended up sprawled on the cottage floor.

The visitor then crossed the room and disappeared through the wall, into the bedroom where the young couple's baby was asleep. The woman immediately ran into the room and snatched up her child but had no further encounter with him there; he had seemingly vanished. She did, however, notice a permeating coldness in that particular room.

On returning to the front room, the young adults felt absolutely terrified and sat huddled together for several hours, with their baby, quite unable to move or sleep. They both truly believed that they had just witnessed a ghost. By now, the whole of the cottage had become freezing cold and suddenly a second noise heralded the return of the spectral fisherman. The horrified couple thus witnessed him emerge from the bedroom wall and cross the room towards the front door, through which he simply walked, without opening it. When the couple reached the door seconds later, they quickly opened it and looked outside. The figure had disappeared into thin air so they both returned inside. The cottage had mysteriously become much warmer and neither of them now felt afraid.

The Evidence

This story is fascinating, yet not a one-off. A previous owner of the same cottage had also experienced an identical manifestation some years before, whilst an even earlier owner had often sensed a presence at night and inexplicable drops in temperature in certain places. Sure enough, the authors' research revealed that a fisherman had been a previous owner of the property for many years and by habit would often return home late at night. He would then leave the house early in the morning to start work on his boat. It is known that he had died in the cottage shortly before the commencement of the strange occurrences.

On continuing to investigate, the authors discovered that such 'haunting' stories, associated with spectral fishermen, are far from uncommon in the village of Newlyn. Sudden loss of life in the brave fishing community, by drowning or other accident, is all too frequent and the ghosts of these unfortunate victims of the deep are often loathe to depart this earth, and so return to their former homes and terrify the subsequent owners.

The Location

(SW463286)

Since the householders of this tale have requested confidentiality, the exact location of this haunted cottage cannot be revealed. However, the old part of the village, from the new fish market to Chywoone (or Paul) Hill, behind the old ice works, contains many tightly packed dwellings, some with their own ghost story, the one above being a typical example. The streets here do merit a slow stroll for any visitor keen to absorb the atmosphere of a Victorian fishing village, which is still palpable in these narrow streets with their almost overcrowded lifestyle.

NEWLYN OLD TOWN: In these typical narrow streets, several phantoms of drowned sailors have been encountered by residents.

THE PORTHGWARRA SWEETHEARTS

In the eighteenth century, the hamlet of Porthgwarra (known then as Pargwarra) was situated on a particularly remote cove and separated from surrounding villages by tiny lanes winding over the granite landscape. Porthgwarra today is a small fishing cove of rugged beauty and possesses a long sandy channel for boats to reach the steep beach. Extensive beds of treacherous, razor-sharp rocks fill the rest of the area beneath the cliffs.

It was here that William, the son of a fisherman, was born. As a youth, he was apprenticed to a local farmer at Roskestal Farm (SW372224). Whilst in this employ, William formed a deep and lasting relationship with the farmer's daughter, Nancy. In turn she was hopelessly devoted to her strong, handsome, young boyfriend. In summer, William, by tradition, left to work for the fishing fleet, always to return to the farm each winter when fisher folk lived on shore, owing to the ferocity of the winter storms.

Nancy's parents, however, were less than happy with their daughter's relationship and whilst William was away, they both tried their utmost, with threats and promises, to dissuade their daughter from her feelings towards a man who in their opinion was socially inferior. Nancy refused to agree and such was her love that she became ill with longing and concern for William's safe return.

Later that year, when William arrived back at the farm, he was ordered off the premises and told never to return by Nancy's parents. But Nancy pined so much that her father offered a compromise, suggesting that William should go to sea the following summer for a period of three years, to make his fortune. Then after such a time, if the young couple remained so in love, they would be permitted to marry.

William and Nancy were both deeply unwilling to accept this arrangement, but realised that there would be no alternative. On the night of William's departure, he pledged himself in secret to Nancy and they performed a powerful old Celtic marriage ritual, swearing undying love to each other. Hands were joined under living spring water and a gold ring was halved, the lovers keeping one piece each to remind them of their unbreakable oath. Finally, a small fire was lit on the local Garrack Zaus, or Holy Rock, and with their hands still entwined they called on the spirits of air and sea to witness their undying union.

Next day the couple parted, William to a merchant ship for three years and Nancy back to her father's farm, to await her love's return. The girl was constantly encouraged by her mother to meet the sons of suitable local gentry and to forget about William, but she always refused such meetings.

Three long years passed and by that winter there was still no sign of William's ship. Nancy was beginning to lose both hope and sanity. She took to wandering the Porthgwarra cliffs by day and night, watching for the sails of William's vessel. There is a sheltered grassy spot on the cliff top of Hella Point, which overlooks Porthgwarra Cove, where Nancy was said to lie waiting for her lover to return. 'Sweet Nancy's Bed', as the place became known, was a dangerous location from which one could easily slip and fall over the cliff's edge. So her mother arranged for Nancy's aunt, Prudence, to follow the girl and guard her safety.

SWEET NANCY'S BED, HELLA POINT: Co-author Geoff with his dogs Dougal and Jake.

One cold moonlit night that winter, Prudence and Nancy were in bed. Nancy was in her usual withdrawn and melancholic state. Suddenly, William's voice was heard beneath the bedroom window calling out to 'sweet Nancy'. Prudence heard the voice asking Nancy to come with him to the cove and his awaiting boat. Without hesitation, the girl replied, 'I'll be with thee in an instant,' and after hurriedly dressing, she left the room, followed a little later by Prudence.

Prudence had noticed that William seemed deathly pale, his clothes dripping with water. She began to fear for Nancy's safety as the two lovers moved quickly along the short cut to the cove. Prudence walked a short distance behind them and from the cliff top soon caught sight of Nancy and William moving effortlessly across the flat rocks in the cove, and reaching a large boat moored beside the entrance to the channel. Then dense swirling mists arose and hid the couple from sight. After a few moments they cleared but both the boat and lovers had gone. Suddenly, Prudence could hear beautiful, melodic singing coming from the cove. Locally such singing was associated with mermaids and the coming of severe weather.

At daybreak, William's father awoke and remembered that during the night he had experienced the most vivid of dreams about his son William, where he was told of his return. So intense had been this vision that he immediately journeyed to Nancy's farm to ask after his son, since he felt that William must have returned to claim his beautiful bride. The farmer told the fisherman of the story of his daughter's rendezvous with the drenched and pale-faced sailor, and William's father returned to his cottage, saddened at missing his son.

That afternoon a storm blew up and a young sailor came to William's cottage. The father was told that William's merchant ship had docked the previous day at the Mount harbour, and that his son, whilst furling a sail, had fallen into the sea from the mast top and been drowned.

Soon, it became evident that William's ghost had returned to take sweet Nancy away, as he had promised he would. The two, as flesh and blood, were never seen again. The small village was plunged into mourning and for many years Porthgwarra was known as the 'Sweethearts' Cove'.

PORTHGWARRA COVE: Nancy's farm, Roskestal, lies over the left skyline. The tall black cleft in the cliffs on the left, is reputed to be a former smugglers' tunnel. Note the narrow sea channel where William's phantom ship is supposed to have entered.

The Evidence

Over a period of three centuries many people have claimed to hear mermaids singing before a storm, and some to have seen the pathetic wraith of Nancy on Hella Point, apparently re-enacting her vigil for her lover William. The cove has always been a place of intense environmental beauty, as well as being wild and dangerous during an Atlantic storm. The sandy channel entrance to the beach, where William's boat was said to have moored in wait for him and Nancy, is still present. Even Roskestal Farm exists nearby, in a hamlet, about three-quarters of a mile from the cove. Thus, there are many elements of fact which help to give credence to the tragic account. However, if you should walk the headland at night on Hella Point, west of the cove, do not confuse the low moaning noise out at sea with the song of the mermaid. It is far more likely to be the constant tidal movement through the Runnelstone Buoy,

PORTHGWARRA COVE, LOOKING OUT TO SEA: This dramatic view is taken from Nancy's Path to Hella Point.

moored in the Channel. Mermaid song, almost surely, would be far more inspiring and heart-rending!

Location

From Land's End (SW342253) take the B3315 towards Treen and the Logan Rock. After about 1½ miles you come to an acute right-hand bend, in a hamlet named Polgigga. Leave the B road here and travel on to the narrow road marked 'Porthgwarra'. You will pass several farms and within half a mile you will reach the buildings of Roskestal Farm, where Nancy lived. The road becomes extremely narrow and winds on to Porthgwarra Cove. Here you will see a large grassy car park.

William and Nancy would have often walked in similar footsteps over this area, particularly along the straight downhill footpath from the farm, across fields and to the cove itself.

ROSKESTAL FARM, PORTHGWARRA: Home of Nancy. Here the deceased William was said to have returned to claim his sweetheart.

Hella Point (SW371214), Nancy's frequent lookout and haunt, lies west of the cove via a footpath past a public convenience. On a warm sunny day, this headland, cove and the surrounding cliffs are glorious. They are ideal for walking, sunbathing or just enjoying the beauty. Indeed this region should be recommended to any visitor to Cornwall. If you do pay a visit and stand on the edge looking out across the rolling sea, empty your mind and try to imagine the scene, 300 years ago. This would have been a remote and under-developed place. Picture a driving winter rainstorm and a beautiful young girl standing on the grassy precipice, gazing to sea and pining for her missing lover. Here lies the beauty of Cornwall's environmental magic, mixed with glorious folk-tales.

Map, reference to:

1 'Sweet Nancy's Bed' (Porthgwarra Sweethearts) (see p.67)
2 William and Nancy's departure point
3 Madge Figgy, Witch and Wrecker – The Chair (see p.119)
4 William and Nancy's short cut to cove
5 Nancy's Farm (Roskestal)

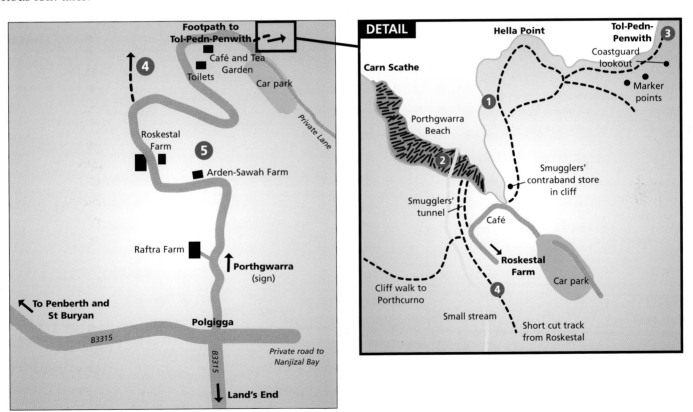

PISTOL MEADOW

On the south-west side of the rugged Lizard peninsula lies a poignant and forgotten area of twisted willow and scrub. This meadow on a rocky headland holds the remains of a macabre and horrifying event and is known locally as Pistol (Pistil) Meadow. The Lizard itself is surmounted by the lighthouse station, which for many years has warned passing ships away from the certain destruction awaiting them on its undersea reefs. Viewed from its furthest point, the sullen grey Atlantic tears its surface on the deadly line of sharp black rocky teeth. In past years the dense swirling sea fogs to which this region is prone, when accompanied by gale and driving rain, have caused numerous unfortunate vessels to founder around these shores.

These dangerous local waters are epitomised by the following account; both for the manner of death and for the terrible pathos of the sequence of events.

PISTOL COVE, LIZARD POINT: The dark brooding razor-sharp rocks at the entrance to Pistol Cove, which claimed the lives of over 200 shipwrecked soldiers.

In about 1750, one of several British transport ships sailing out from England, filled with soldiers for the Peninsular War in Spain, was driven on to a submerged reef close to Lizard Point. It started sinking rapidly, with catastrophic loss of life. One simply needs to visit this remote place on a wild December day, with clouds of icy Atlantic spray shrouding the headlands, to understand the sheer horror of the predicament of the soldiers and crew. By morning light the resultant slaughter was revealed, showing over 200 mangled and wasted corpses strewn over the cove beneath Pistol Meadow. Local residents discovered the grim remains at low water, jammed into rocky crevices, some half-buried under the sand thrown up by the storm. They also discovered a large cache of pistols, which had been part of the cargo of this wrecked troop ship.

The path to the cove is extremely steep and hazardous, as found in earlier explorations! It descends via a treacherous, narrow, winding path, over 100 feet to the rocks and beach below. Obviously this mass of corpses needed burial, though consecrated ground was out of the question for shipwreck victims. The able-bodied of the Lizard began the dreadful task of lifting the mangled remains to a hastily dug mass shallow grave, in the cliff-top meadow above the cove. This gruesome mission took several days of very hard labour in order to lay each poor soul to rest. Towards the end of the interment, many of the corpses still lay decomposing, and large packs of stray dogs were feeding on and mutilating the rotting flesh. Almost a week passed before committal of the dead had been completed, and the grave covered about 500 square feet. It is marked today by a small enclosure, bordered with misshapen, stumpy willows and covered with rough hillocks. The meadow itself is far from being lush green pasture but is a wild wind-scorched and desolate place, covering the horror beneath its surface.

PISTOL COVE FROM THE CLIFFS ABOVE: The soldiers' mangled corpses were strewn across this dramatic setting.

PISTOL MEADOW AND WILLOW ENCLOSURE: Over 200 souls found their last resting place here. Most were buried under the copse, the rest on the meadow land to the left. A melancholic hush still rests heavily on the area.

It is claimed that for years after this tragic event, dogs were never seen at the Lizard Point and surrounding area, so revolted were the locals by the stray dogs' behaviour. Indeed, any visiting pet hound was made distinctly unwelcome. Travel diaries written between 1750 and 1850 have documented the marked absence of dogs, and even now there are not as many as would usually be expected.

The Evidence

The authors have not found any authentic record of an actual ghost or visual re-enactment of this drama. Pistol Meadow is rather a place of eerie atmosphere and many have claimed to be overcome with feeling of melancholy, even despair. You may think that this emotion would be anyone's natural reaction in the grey of winter, but perhaps not on a bright June afternoon. For those readers who might consider the time of year to be major factor, the author would like to relate this simple but true story of his own experiences at Pistol Meadow.

In 1983, with my wife and dog, I came across Pistol Meadow, by purely chance encounter on one of our rambles. We had been searching for an access to the cliffs via the village and finally parked in a grassy lay-by alongside a sunken path descending across meadows. Our little dog, a Yorkshire terrier named Samantha, always accompanied us on our treks, as was the case that day. It was a bright summer afternoon yet, unbeknown to us, all was set for an unexpected brush with the unexplained.

As soon as we parked and opened the car door, Samantha became terrified and ran under the car, refusing to budge. Eventually she was extracted and, still shaking, was put on a lead for a stroll. She had to be carried along the lane to the cliffs since she refused to walk forwards. Eventually we reached an incredibly twisted enclosure of willows on the cliff's edge, without knowing of Pistol Meadow at this time. The dog seemed to sense something which we clearly could not and, as we let her off the lead, still shaking, we were hoping to descend to the cove below. Samantha, however, had other ideas and with a yelp fled across the adjoining fields as if the Devil himself was in pursuit. She was found some twenty minutes later, hiding in a hedge near our car. Nothing ever explained her behaviour and refusal to visit what later proved to be Pistol Meadow. Nor did she ever behave like that before or after the event. Could this little dog have picked up the contempt for 'man's best friend' that had apparently been so strong for over a hundred years up until about 1900, or did she fear the atmosphere of the place, with its mass grave and other secrets?

It was in 1989, almost six years later, that we read of Pistol Meadow and began to draw our own conclusions to our experience. Samantha died in 1986, and with her the strange reasons for her uncharacteristic behaviour. Perhaps the ghost seekers with their own pet dogs will be in for an equally strange encounter if they venture to this same, sad location.

Location

Pistol Meadow lies at grid reference SW694127.

BRIDLEWAY SIGN TO PISTOL MEADOW

Fortunately, Pistol Meadow is easier to find today, thanks to new signposting. However, it is a hazardous, though lovely position on the cliff edge, west of Lizard Point. Walking from the Lizard Point café westwards is difficult, owing to the cliff edge and the wire fencing which bounds the field's perimeter. Alternatively, park west of the village centre and locate the half-mile route to the cliffs, via the narrow lane. It begins on the outer edge of a small housing estate (SW697127) and leads almost directly to the burial ground with its willow trees. A small stream is close by and bubbles across the fields to the cliffs. Descent to the cove depends on the weather and state of the tide.

When you stand in the grave enclosure, please do have respect for what lies a few feet under your shoes. You may well feel the suffocating mantle of despair and unbroken hush which is said to be experienced without warning, by many

Map, reference to:

Pistol Meadow

of those who dare to visit. The authors returned here during the writing of the book and were both struck by the unearthly silence. It was like no other and quickly penetrated the soul.

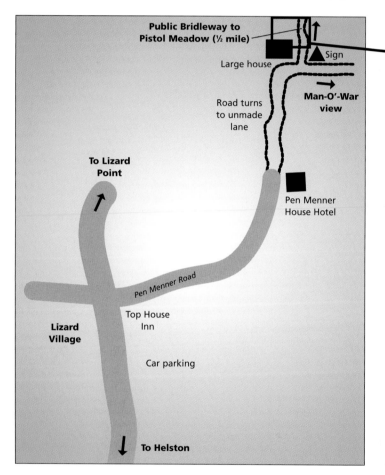

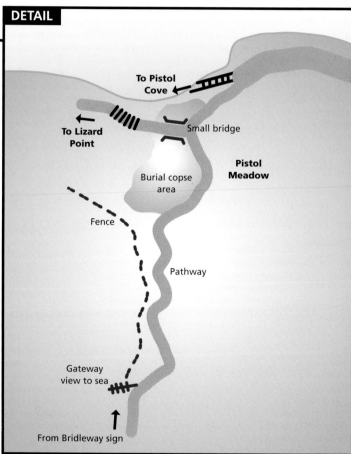

THE SEAMEN'S MORGUE AND OTHER GHOSTS, PORTREATH

Lying north of Camborne is the harbour village of Portreath. The town is popular with surfers and water enthusiasts of many kinds and is enjoyed by numerous visitors each year. It was traditionally a fishing village and many of its former dwellings were typical fishermen's huts. However, most of these were demolished some years ago to be replaced with more modern housing. In particular, the area around the harbour boasts several attractive modern buildings and houses spreading out from the waterside. Many of these properties are situated directly on top of older sites, whose buildings often had an interesting tale attached.

Some years ago, for example, it was claimed that the Smuggler's Cottage Guest House had long been haunted. The ghost was believed to be a ghoulish man in his twenties; his clothing resembled the Jacobean style and everything about him seemed 'not of our era'. He had been seen on numerous occasions, especially on the stairs and on the first floor. He was usually preceded by a pronounced drop in temperature, described as being 'like walking into an industrial freezer'. Any animals which entered the building soon started to act strangely, staring at an empty space or behaving nervously. Indeed, dogs always seemed to be seen growling at the same empty spot on the stairs. Whether or not this was one of the smugglers who appeared in the name of the establishment is unknown but the ghost certainly caused a great deal of anxiety at the guest house.

There is another building in Portreath with its own fascinating stories. Situated on the sea front, it seems to have its own resident spectres. These too seem to cause more than their fair share of fear among residents and visitors to Portreath. Where the building stands today was originally a large storage hut. This was used for many different purposes over the years, from storing coal to keeping fishing gear and boat parts. However, at some point the building had been requisitioned for an altogether more sinister purpose – as a makeshift morgue. Any bodies which were discovered on the beach,

DEADMAN'S HUT, PORTREATH: This isolated round hut, similar to the one outlined in the story 'The Seamen's Morgue', is situated at the top of a steep flight of steps. It is also said to retain a sinister atmosphere.

thrown up by the relentless sea, were brought here for storage until someone came to claim the corpse.

As the years went by, many unfortunate souls claimed by the 'cruel widow maker' found themselves unceremoniously dumped in the building. It was common for a body to be left there for quite some time, especially if the family could not be traced. Worse still, some of the victims of the sea were never claimed, let alone identified. These poor creatures would be buried in a pauper's grave, without pomp or ceremony, with nobody to mourn their passing, and their grave would be marked with the sad, stark inscription 'unknown seaman'.

Ghost stories are made from such tales, so it is little surprise that the present-day location is believed to be haunted by a ghost or ghosts assumed to be one or more of these hapless sailors, who so ignominuously ended their days here. A man in very strange, old-fashioned clothing has been seen on several occasions in the new building, which for many years has been a restaurant, near the water's edge. He is described as being of average height, looking forlorn and somewhat 'misty'. Most people have actually described him as being peculiarly transparent. His identity, like so many of the bodies brought to the original building, remains a mystery but it does seem a fair bet that he is the spirit of one of them. Perhaps he is still distraught at not receiving a proper Christian service before his burial all those years ago.

The Evidence

In the 1970s, one female customer of the restaurant reported what seemed to be a very clear sighting. As she ate her meal, she glanced up to see a 'misty form' standing in the corner of the room. The figure was clearly a man and was wearing clothing from another era. Despite this, she was staggered to find that she could see almost straight through him, and indeed was so shocked that she immediately left the restaurant, her meal unfinished, refusing to ever return again.

The business has gone through many changes and several refurbishments, and the ghost has often made its presence known at such times.

In the mid-1980s, while the kitchen was being improved, this figure appeared again, standing in the doorway. He could be seen for several minutes by two stunned workmen, and then simply vanished. The last definite sighting was just a few years ago, by a young girl working at the restaurant. She claimed to see the ghost on several occasions, although nobody else was present, and she often felt a peculiar feeling, likened to the touch of an icy hand.

Location

Portreath can be reached by following the A30 and turning on to the B3300, near Redruth. Follow the signs for Portreath. The sea front and beaches are clearly visible (SW657454). There is a similar 'Deadman's Hut', itself linked to strange phenomena and deep sadness, situated on the harbour and located in the map.

In addition, there is another story related to Portreath and a 'spooky' morgue. At nearby RAF Portreath, there is said to be a very long corridor with a room at the top. Many people have been in this corridor and have reported feeling very uncomfortable, particularly as they approach the room. Indeed, several of them have been so unnerved they have refused to enter the room. Many believe that it has retained something of its unpleasant former use. It is as if the atmosphere of death still lingers there, because this was indeed the morgue.

Map, reference to:

The Seamen's Morgue and other Ghosts

PLAQUE BELOW DEADMAN'S HUT, PORTREATH

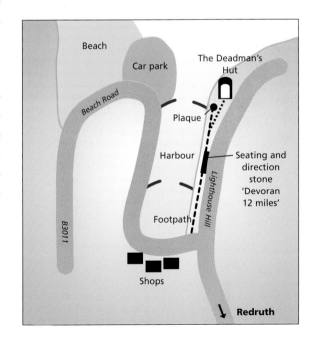

DEADMAN'S COVE

On the Godrevy to Portreath Heritage coast lies the alarmingly titled 'Deadman's Cove'. It has often been said that a mysterious figure, dressed from head to foot in black, has been seen here. The figure appears to be a tall man, exuding an extremely sinister countenance. There are no clues to his identity, and it seems he wishes to keep it that way, because anyone who has been brave enough to approach him has immediately seen him miraculously disappear. It seems very likely that he is in some way linked to the smuggling activity once so prevalent in this part of Cornwall. Perhaps he is a smuggler who came to a sticky end or, alternatively, a victim of a cutthroat band who wronged them in some way. The imagination could easily run away!

TREACHEROUS CLIFFS NEAR DEADMAN'S COVE, PORTREATH: The imposing haunt of a ghostly black figure, said to be one of a notorious band of cutthroat smugglers. The photograph was taken with Portreath lying in the background (see map p.38).

The Evidence

There would appear to be on average at least one sighting every year, some-times more. Many of those who later claim to have seen the figure, seem to have no prior knowledge of him. It can be assumed, therefore, that auto-suggestion or hypersensitivity may be ruled out.

Location

Deadman's Cove lies on the coast (SW613432), less than 2 miles along the B3011 from Portreath to Hayle. Standing here looking out over the dramatic seascape can be inspiring and one's imagination can quickly drift, conjuring up images of smugglers, ancient ships and characters from centuries long past. At what stage does imagination become reality?

THE SEAMAN'S GHOST OF ZENNOR

The romantic and picturesque village of Zennor is steeped in tradition and folklore; a quick visit to the Wayside Folklore Museum tells you as much. The place could have fallen straight out of a Victorian novel about a typical Cornish village. It stands intriguingly between rugged cliffs and rolling moor, and is a beautiful spot to live in, or visit. Zennor's history is full of myth and sagas that fire the imagination, not least the legend of the mermaid. Another one of the classics is the story of the seaman's ghost; a sad yet poignant tale of true friendship.

In the early part of the nineteenth century a man named James Bottrell came to live at Zennor, after finishing his long distinguished career at sea. However, his planned retirement to an easy and peaceful life was soon thwarted by events. Poor James found himself plagued by the ghost of a fellow sailor, desperate for his help. It all began early one morning after a particularly fierce winter's night. James was startled awake by three loud knocks coming from his bedroom window. As he glanced up from his bed, he was astonished to see a man standing by his bedside. Soon his surprise turned to fear as the realisation hit him that he was face to face with a former shipmate who had already died. Here was the phantom form of John Jones, his best friend from his former ship, standing there surrounded by an aura of light, both strange and mystical.

But his old friend was not as he remembered him. Before him now stood a 'wreck' of the former man; he appeared to be pale and a miserable expression was etched across his face. James lay there transfixed by this apparition, knowing not what to do, until suddenly his friend just disappeared. James simply could not believe his eyes, though eventually he convinced himself that he must have imagined the glowing spectre.

The next night the same thing happened again. The ghostly form of John Jones stood directly over him, not speaking and unmoving. Over the next week the visitations became regular; every night in the early hours the sad apparition appeared again, yet never spoke. Then more strange things began to occur. There were peculiar sounds heard throughout the house, even in the daytime, and other disturbances that could not be rationalised. To James's mounting horror, after another week, the ghostly form of his old comrade began appearing yet more frequently, at other times and in other places. It was as if he was becoming more desperate to appeal to James on some urgent matter. Sometimes, even in the daytime he would turn to see John Jones standing there, looking directly at him with an angry look fixed upon his face.

Eventually James became distraught and did not know what to do with himself for fear of this strange ghost. He finally spoke to some friends, who advised him to attempt to communicate with the ghost. They suggested that a friend, ghost or not, would surely wish him no harm and must have something very important to tell him. They also told him that a ghost could not speak first and so he must overcome his fear and make the first move, to avoid incurring his friend's displeasure.

At the next visitation, James summoned up the resolve to talk to him and said, 'Tell me, John Jones, what shall I do to give thee rest?'

John replied, 'It is well thou hast spoken, for I should have been the death of thee if thou hadst much longer refused to speak. What grieved and vexed me most was to see that thou seemedst to fear thy old comrade, who always liked thee best of all his shipmates.'

The two old pals began a long conversation and James was certainly no longer afraid of his friend's apparition. It was not long before he learned why his friend was unable to rest in peace. John Jones had been on board a ship in the Bay of Biscay when rough seas began tossing the boat. Poor John slipped and fell straight overboard and had drowned before anyone had noticed him missing. Such a sudden end had prevented him from sorting out his affairs and much of his money had been left in a chest, which was now in storage at an inn in the port of Plymouth in Devon. Indeed, this was the place that the two shipmates always drank together, when they came back from sea. John wanted his friend to proceed to Plymouth to collect his trunk and pay off his debts. For this favour he could keep the rest of the money for himself. James swiftly agreed to this one last favour and the deal was made. For the first time John smiled, then vanished with the grin still etched upon his face.

The next morning James procured a horse and set off on the long journey through Cornwall. It took him two full days and on arrival in Plymouth he bedded down at the inn. That night John's ghost appeared again. James had been wondering how he would convince the inn's landlady to allow him to take the chest but John soon reassured him. The landlady knew them well as friends and did not know that John had been drowned. He therefore suggested that James tell her he was in town (technically true) and would see her directly but that he had been sent ahead to collect his trunk for him.

As it turned out the landlady was happy to oblige and sent her 'love' to 'Captain Jones', as she always called him. She pleaded with James to beg that

John come to see her before returning to sea. James duly opened the chest and under John's direction found the money in a secret compartment. He then set out with John at his side to settle his friend's debts. Once the final payment had been made, John disappeared again and James set off for a look at the docks (now Devonport). He was busy looking at the ships and so failed to see John return. When he did notice him, a change seemed to have come over him. He looked very different from their last meeting, appearing much younger and happier, and was clothed in a fine new sailor's outfit, looking just as James remembered him from when they were last at sea together. It was as if this last deed had returned him to his former self. John informed him that he had paid a visit to the landlady and had now come to bid him farewell and thank him for his kindness.

'My dearest Jim, I will now bid thee farewell. I'm off to sea again, for, with an occasional trip to the Green, I know no way of passing the time that better suits me. Thou wilt never more see me whilst thou art alive, but if thou thinkest of me at the hour of death we shall meet, as soon as the breath leaves thy body. When thine is laid in Zennor churchyard we will rove the seas together again.'

Moments later, before James could speak, John's ghost could be seen heading aboard a ship and disappearing once again. James, with sorrow in his heart, mournfully turned and set off for the long journey back to Zennor, all the time thinking of his friend. James lived out the rest of his days there, untroubled, and was indeed laid in Zennor churchyard. People tell that when he lay on his deathbed an apparition appeared in the room and as he died, the ghost, believed to be that of John Jones, vanished.

The Evidence

Inevitably with such a story, there simply are no modern sightings at all. However, the avid ghost hunter need not be disappointed as Zennor does have several other ghosts, who do seem to be active today. On the edge of the village is a winding lane (begins SW456383) leading to a farm (Foage), and is a place best avoided at night by those with a nervous disposition as many have reported a dark presence. Others have actually claimed to see the ghost of a man walking up the lane in Victorian clothes, pushing a bicycle and covered in blood. Horses have been known to panic, dogs react aggressively, and there is often a strange feeling of being watched. At a cottage near the lane a female ghost, described as friendly, also resides.

A 'Miller's Cottage' over 200 years old is also believed to be haunted by a more sinister presence and the building is said to be enveloped in sadness.

The Tinner's Arms public house (SW453385) is believed to have been haunted for as long as anyone can remember. Mysterious footsteps have been heard at night, dogs often bark for no reason, glasses have been smashed and objects have moved by themselves. This 'poltergeist' activity becomes prevalent before a thunderstorm.

Location

The beautiful village of Zennor (SW454385) is found by taking the B3306 from St Ives and following the signs straight into Zennor itself. Fuller directions can be found in the 'Mermaid of Zennor' story.

THE SAILOR'S GHOST, PENZANCE

The following is an account of a classic ghostly tale of murder, treachery and stolen treasure at Penzance.

At the beginning of the nineteenth century, Quay Street in Penzance was one of the most fashionable parts of the town. Located by the harbour it contained many exclusive and large houses. The street bore witness to much of the town's growth in trade and maritime success and was frequented by all manner of seafarers. But one of the houses soon developed a reputation for being haunted. Indeed it was told that several people had independently alleged that the ghost of a tall young man, appearing to be in an old-style sailor's uniform, would often make a frightening appearance at the property. Soon the locals, being a superstitious bunch, no longer ventured near the place and certainly nobody would live there. As a result the house fell into disrepair and became infamous for its disturbing tales. It was known that on occasions locals, especially children, would set foot in the place for some kind of dare. Often they swiftly left, after claiming to have been scared out of their wits. Whether these people were deluded owing to hypersensitivity or had genuinely experienced the supernatural seemed to matter little. The building's notoriety increased.

One evening two young sailors chanced upon the haunted house and realised that the place was standing empty. Their ship was moored in port and rather than spend yet another night in cramped conditions on the boat, the men took their opportunity and broke in. They settled down to rest in one of the upstairs rooms, blissfully unaware of the house's ghoulish reputation, and after a long journey at sea, were asleep in minutes. Before long, both men were awoken with a start. A loud noise had been clearly heard, coming from outside the room. As both men lay there and listened, they soon realised that what had disturbed them were heavy footsteps, heading up the stairs.

Fearing that the owner had entered the property, both men hurriedly began to gather their things, preparing for a quick escape. Nevertheless they were not fast enough because before they knew it somebody entered the room. They looked up and to their dismay, saw a man moving further into the meagre light in the room. However, as he became clearer they saw that he was also dressed in a sailor's uniform. For a brief moment the two men felt relief, thinking it was either a fellow crewman who had come to look for them or a mariner in similar need to their own.

Their curiosity quickly turned to horror as they observed the young 'Jack Tar', solid and clear, cross the room and walk straight through the wall. The two men, almost as one, fled from the room and out of the building. They discussed what they had seen and agreed that neither had been hallucinating. They had both clearly seen a man, who initially seemed to be very substantial, just vanish through a solid wall. They also realised that this young seafarer had been wearing a uniform out of use for several decades. The two petrified men headed for a local tavern for a desperately needed drink and began recounting their experiences to other drinkers. Soon a large group had gathered round, listening to the men. Several of the men present said that they were not remotely surprised by the sailors' tale and confirmed that other sightings had been made which were identical to that of the sailors. It seems the ghost was always described in the same way.

Some years later, in 1813, the house had fallen into such a poor state that it was torn down completely and a startling discovery was made. A skeleton of a man was found walled up in an upstairs room. In fact, the remains were discovered in the same room where the sailors had seen the ghost. The circumstances were clearly suspicious and people soon linked the grisly remains to a former resident, believing that the man had almost certainly been stabbed to death and bricked up in the house. Stories soon circulated about what lay behind the grisly find.

The most persistent story claimed that a young sailor, much travelled, had resided at the property. He had possessed sizeable riches, collected from his travels abroad, and had openly boasted about his treasures. Then, suddenly and mysteriously, he had disappeared with no explanation. Most people assumed he had tired of life on land and had gone off to sea, taking his money with him. Now people believed that the skeleton must have belonged to this sailor and that some unknown malefactor had killed the unfortunate fellow and escaped with his booty.

It seems the ghost most likely belonged to the owner of the skeleton, presumably this rich sailor. It could never be known what had happened or who had killed him in such a despicable way. Perhaps the sailor's spirit was unable to depart, owing to his tragic end. Conceivably, as so many ghosts are claimed to do, he was fated to remain 'earthbound', seeking justice or vengeance or trying to convey to somebody the circumstances of his death. Not for him would it be the Isle of Avalon, the sailor's blessed paradise, but an endless ghostly existence, trapped in pepetual spirit form, and forlornly searching for his former wealth.

The Evidence

When the building was demolished, it might have been expected that the poor sailor's ghost would move on. However, this may not be the case. On the former site of the house now lies a series of smaller, modern tenements owned by a local housing association. Just a short time ago an elderly lady, who lived in one of the properties, insisted that she was being troubled by a resident ghost who was regularly tormenting her. Almost daily she visited the association's office, complaining that her flat was undoubtedly haunted and she wished to be rehoused. Inevitably, perhaps, her insistence was not taken too seriously. It was assumed that she was attempting to engineer a move through devious methods. However, she persisted with her claims of mysterious happenings at the flat.

Not long after this the author had a chance conversation with an employee of the housing association, telling her about the history of the location and giving her some details about the former ghost and other information. She looked taken aback and mentioned the elderly lady and her alleged experiences. The author was able to confirm that her flat would almost certainly have been situated within the boundaries of the original house. This was apparently the first time she had even begun to imagine that the woman's story could be genuine. Perhaps, she considered, it could be the same ghost. The author has no idea if the sailor's ghost is still around or if some other spirit is focused on Quay Street. However, happy to relate, the woman did at last get her move away from the property and her troubles, whether real or not, do seem to be over.

Location

Quay Street is located very close to the harbour in Penzance (SW477299). Drive into Penzance on the A30. Follow the road around to the left into Station Road (past the railway station). From here there are two routes: (1) Stay in the left-hand lane and drive along Wharf Road (car park on your left). Carry on over the bridge (Ross swing-bridge) past the docks on your right and along The Quay until reaching the harbour, which will be on your left. Before the corner turn right (to the right of the Dolphin Tavern) into Quay Street. About halfway up on your right is where the house once stood. (2) Move into the right-hand lane and up Albert Street. Turn into the left lane and into Market Jew Street (town centre). Stay on the main street until you pass the Humphry Davy statue (on your right, in front of the town clock). Take the next left, this leads into Chapel Street and continue down Chapel Street, which leads to Quay Street (map p.43).

SPIRITS AT THE INN, THE DOLPHIN TAVERN, PENZANCE

Remarkably, it seems that there are more pubs with a ghostly story than those without. One cannot go out for a pleasant drink without running the gauntlet of supernatural activity. In particular, there are dozens of Cornish pubs with claims that a visitor from the spirit world is in residence. There are many eye-witness accounts and locals are happy to talk about their ghoulish encounters. A number of such establishments are referred to elsewhere in the book and more information can be found in a forthcoming book by Ian Addicoat entitled *One Too Many Spirits,* about local public houses and their ghosts. Some of the pubs with stories relating to the sea, include: a murdered sailor and smugglers at Jamaica Inn, Bodmin Moor; smugglers at the Napoleon Inn, Boscastle; a smuggler named Finny, killed by revenue officers at the Finnygook Inn, Crafthole; a ghostly sailor at the Ship Inn, Porthleven, and so many more. However, perhaps the most famous ghost story centres on the Dolphin Tavern, Penzance.

THE DOLPHIN TAVERN, PENZANCE: This is an infamous 'haunt' for several spectres, the most famous of which is the sea captain, nicknamed George. The inn has long been a popular location for tourists.

The Dolphin has been featured in many ghostly publications and is a charming hostelry, at the time of writing run by the jovial Bob Mann. It is believed to be haunted by several ghosts but most famously by a 'salty old sea captain'. The pub itself dates back to the sixteenth century and has acquired plenty of colourful history. In particular, smuggling was common here, with many tunnels discovered underneath the building. Also, two hidden rooms were found about a hundred years ago, containing old oak casks full of alcohol. Heavy footsteps and strange dragging noises have often been heard in empty rooms and are inevitably linked to the previous smuggling activity of bygone days. Sir Walter Raleigh was rumoured to have stayed here and possibly smoked tobacco for the first time on British soil. Sir John Hawkins is said to have used the building as an occasional headquarters and the infamous 'Hanging' Judge Jeffreys supposedly used the inn as a courtroom during the Monmouth rebellion.

Nevertheless, the most persistent story refers to the sea captain, nicknamed George. He has made countless appearances and shown his presence in the upstairs part of the building, the cellar and even the main bar. He is described as an elderly man, wearing old-fashioned sailor's clothing, a tricorn hat, and sporting a big bushy beard. Many people have mistaken him for a real person in fancy dress or a quaintly costumed member of staff. His activities are certainly frequent.

The Evidence

This is almost certainly a haunting still persisting today. Several members of staff who are 'sensitive' claim to experience his activities on a weekly basis and many customers have seen or felt him on a regular basis. This has often been without any prior knowledge of him or the story. The author was once speaking with the manager on the phone when 'George' apparently drifted across the bar, according to a barmaid. The author has also heard the footsteps moving across the top floor, and has a copy of a photograph taken at the Dolphin in 2002 showing a very clear orb (said to suggest a ghostly presence). A woman who became a relief manager of the Dolphin for a few weeks, just over five years ago, has also related her experiences. These included all kinds of unexplainable happenings, including doors locking by themselves, spooky feelings, eerie atmospheres, sudden temperature drops, mysterious footsteps, banging and crashing, breakages, feelings of panic and other peculiar phenomena.

Location

The Dolphin lies at the bottom of Quay Street, Penzance, opposite the harbour (SW478298). For full directions, see 'The Sailor's Ghost', Penzance (map p.43).

THE BOATMEN OF PORTHMEOR BEACH, ST IVES

The beautiful town of St Ives has a good ratio of ghosts to the square mile. Indeed, it continued to employ a ghost layer long after most towns had dispensed with the services of such dubious characters. Many of its spooky stories are recounted elsewhere in this book, in other publications and during the authors' St Ives Ghost Walks. However, here is an interesting story, which is less well known, about the western end of Porthmeor Beach.

CARRICK DU POINT, PORTHMEOR BEACH, ST IVES: Several spectral figures have been witnessed here, clambering up the rocks to the cliffs above, having beached their boat beneath.

On separate occasions people have seen a small boat beach itself and reveal a group of bearded men, wearing long cloaks. They disembark and head for the cliffs at Carrick Du point. The men always seem to follow the same pattern, which may suggest that this particular apparition is a recorded vision, perhaps imprinted on the granite cliffs, as mooted in the Stone Tape theory of paranormal psychology.

The men are observed to be talking animatedly, though no sounds are heard, then they walk to the cliff and begin clambering up the rocks. When they reach the top they stop, form a huddle and look as if they are deep in prayer. At this point they are said to completely vanish, without warning.

Whether this is a religious group, perhaps Celtic saints disembarking from Ireland, or maybe a group of unusually reverent smugglers or fishermen is unclear. There have been independent sightings. Two such appearances were to a Mrs Clare and a Mrs Day, described by Peter Underwood in his book *Ghosts of Cornwall*.

The Evidence

The last definite sighting of these figures reported to the author was in 1993 by a couple on holiday. As they were walking across some rocks in the area of Porthmeor Beach, they were shocked to observe events exactly as just described. They claim to have watched for several minutes, as the group went through their ritual, and were extremely unnerved by their experience. Apparently there have been numerous other witnesses with no prior knowledge of the story.

Location

Drive into St Ives on the A3074, turn left into Gabriel Street (follow the car park sign) and drive past the cinema on the left. At the roundabout turn right into Bullan's Lane, then right again into Teetotal Street. Here turn left on to Porthmeor Hill and follow the steep road down to the bottom where you will see Porthmeor Beach ahead of you. Turn right and look for a car park on the left. Park up and walk back, following the path next to the beach. Take the public footpath on to the cliffs and you will be standing on Carrick Du (SW513410). Look towards the beach and you never know!... (map p.57).

Strange Ladies

The Lady and the Lantern – St Ives
The Irish Lady – Sennen
Sarah Polgrean – Ludgvan
The Grey Lady – St Michael's Mount
The Mermaid of Lamorna – Lamorna Cove
Lutey and the Mermaid – Berepper Sands
The Mermaid of Zennor – Zennor
Madge Figgy – Land's End

THE LADY AND THE LANTERN, ST IVES

One of the most famous, and possibly most persistent, ghost stories in Cornwall is the famous 'white lady' believed to haunt an area of the Island in St Ives. There are several slightly different versions of the tale, each with its own slight inconsistencies. However, the resounding fact is that countless people claim to have seen this particular apparition over a substantial period of time. The most commonly told story suggests that some time ago, during a ferocious storm, a ship got into difficulties as it entered St Ives Bay. With the boat clearly in distress, many local fishing boats bravely headed out to offer assistance. As dusk fell, the fishermen began to lift people off the stricken boat into their own craft. Then tragically, as one young woman was being passed across with her infant baby, the child slipped from her grasp and plummeted into the raging waters, evidently to its doom. The woman was understandably devastated and on arriving at the shore, immediately set out to search the coastline in a desperate, but ultimately vain, hunt for her beloved lost child. The search continued day and night for several days. The forlorn lady carrying a flickering lantern was seen night after night, slowly stumbling across the rocks surrounding the Island. Ultimately the poor woman's desperation gave way to grief and despair, as she realised that her search was destined to fail.

Her utter hopelessness led to her own demise for she perished with a broken heart, her loss too much to bear.

It is claimed that this unfortunate woman was buried in Barnoon cemetery (SW515407), overlooking Porthmeor Beach, but unfortunately her name has never been recorded to enable further research. It would seem, though, that her soul was not at rest, for it was said that no sooner had her body been interred than her ghost rose and began to haunt the Island. Many believed they had encountered it late at night, and it was difficult to assume that this was any other than the tragic lady who had just passed away. Often, particularly on stormy nights, a mysterious light could be spotted slowly flitting across the rocks, mostly on the eastern side of the Island. Anyone who investigated closer claimed to see a young lady dressed all in white, carrying a lighted lantern as if searching for something on the rocks. Yet if anybody approached her, the mysterious figure would suddenly vanish, to the witness's utter astonishment. The sightings became so common that a rock in the vicinity became known as 'Lamp Rock' and is still so-named today.

Another version claims that the ghost belongs to a woman who fell to her death whilst walking late at night on the Island. However, it is the first story which has appeared in print more frequently, perhaps due to the nature of the tale. In yet another version, claims are made that the white lady is seen in the vicinity of St Nicholas' Chapel, also on the Island. Indeed, one superstition states that if you walk right around the chapel at midnight (either three or 12 times, depending on the version) the ghost will appear. Incidentally, the ghost of a monk is also claimed to have been seen going into the chapel on occasions, through the locked door. In the 1940s there was a persistent story about the phantoms of a horse and headless rider seen patrolling the Island late at night, although there have certainly been no recent sightings of them.

Unfortunately there is insufficient historical information available to establish the identity of the lamp lady, or whose ghost has been so frequently sighted, or what may have caused her death. However, it would seem that there is

Above: *THE ISLAND, ST IVES: This is a popular attraction for tourists. The photograph shows the coastguard lookout station and nearby building.*

Left: *ST NICHOLAS' CHAPEL AND THE ISLAND, ST IVES: It is here on the Island that the sad figure of a lady carrying a lantern is said to continue her sorrowful search for her lost baby.*

enough evidence to suggest a strange phenomenon occurring in the area of the Island. An abundance of people claim to have seen the figure or, more frequently, the strange light. Many have approached the light in an attempt to identify it, only to see it mysteriously disappear. Is it a ghostly lamp? Jack Harry's lanterns (see p.132)? Natural energy line? Moonlight? Or perhaps ball lightning? Can any of these give at least some explanation? Certainly the mystery persists to this day.

It is widely believed that the lady and the lamp is an omen for fishermen. If the light appears over the Island rocks, it is supposed to mean tragedy. It is then likely that a storm will follow and disaster will strike somewhere in St Ives Bay.

The Evidence

Many people, both local and visitors, claim to have seen the strange light during the last few years. On some occasions, it can be assumed that natural phenomena may be responsible for certain of the appearances; for example torches, the moon shimmering on the rocks, and the like. However, some cases stand up to better scrutiny. Many witnesses apparently have had no prior knowledge of any accounts about a ghost or strange light, yet many have later reported seeing it. During a St Ives Ghost Walk in July 2001 over 20 people (including the author) collectively saw a flickering light slowly moving across the rocks. The group immediately headed back across the Island to investigate. The light could still be viewed as they neared it, but on arrival at the edge of the rocks (on the eastern side) it suddenly vanished without explanation. There was absolutely no one on the rocks and no apparent cause. In fact this has recurred several times since at the same place, usually on windy nights.

Location

The Island (or St Ives Head) is situated on the north-east of St Ives (SW 522412). Drive into St Ives on the A3074 and go into the town centre via Tregenna Hill. Follow the road right into High Street and then turn right again into Wharf Road. Carry on along the Wharf until you see signs for the car park. Follow these down Island Road until you reach the Island car park. From here you can clearly see the Island. The best location to sight the light, or the lady, is found by walking on to the Island itself and following the path around the perimeter (best avoided during poor conditions). Alternatively walk down past Porthgwidden Beach and look across towards the eastern side of the rocks (SW522410). The chapel of St Nicholas is clearly visible on the Island's summit (map p.57).

THE IRISH LADY

This particularly sad tale comes from the tip of Cornwall and concerns the tragic 'Irish Lady'. Many years ago, a ship sailing from Ireland around the Cornish coast was wrecked just off Sennen. A terrible tempest had blown up and driven the vessel on to the rocks. Everyone on board was lost and drowned at sea, except one young woman. She was miraculously washed on to the large pinnacle of rocks at Pedn-mên-Du, near Sennen. There she desperately and resolutely clung to a rock, and gradually pulled herself up the cliff, only to find her way was barred and she could go no further.

She remained there for days, hanging on grimly for life, unable to move forward and trapped by the waves below. Day by day, any chance of survival faded, yet she lasted for several days against the cruel winds and the intense cold, which in the end overcame her. With her strength gone, thirst, hunger, hypothermia and sheer exhaustion won. The pathetic figure, wearing only a thin white dress, collapsed on to the rocks, her lifeless body lying limp against the cold grey granite cliffs.

Some stories claim that several local people saw her helpless figure, but were unable to cross the perilous cliff or reach her by a boat from below in the terrible storm. Others suggest that her body was found on the rocks and no one had known about her plight. Either way, all stories claim that her wretched soul still haunts the area to this day. On particularly stormy nights, she is seen wearing the same white dress, once again desperately clinging to the rock now known as the Irish Lady.

The Evidence

Many locals claim that this maiden is spotted regularly, but the authors have been unable to trace any witness. It would seem that the person seeing the ghost is always a friend of a friend or a second cousin who has now left the area! But the legend persists, and on dark, stormy nights on the cliffs near Sennen, imagination and reality could perhaps become one!

Location

Take the A30 to Sennen village and turn right down the hill into Sennen Cove. Descend the steep hill and go along the front, past the lifeboat station, and park in the small car park by the jetty (SW351265), space permitting. Walk in a north-westerly direction up the steep incline towards the coastguard lookout on Pedn-mên-Du. Proceed approximately 400 yards further past the lookout station and there below you is the Irish Lady rock, tucked beneath the cliffs (SW346261). (Maps p.63 and p.124).

SARAH POLGREAN (POLGREEN), LUDGVAN

This story is a much related and sinister narrative about forbidden love, murder and mystery, which could readily stand alongside dark gothic tales by the likes of Edgar Allan Poe, Sheridan le Fanu and M.R. James. The overriding message of the story is: 'Be careful what you promise; you never know when it may come back to haunt you.'

In the early part of the eighteenth century a young woman named Sarah Polgrean lived in the village of Ludgvan, near Penzance. She was married to a cantankerous fellow, whose terrible temper was matched only by the hatred growing inside Sarah towards her husband. Sarah began an illicit relationship with a man also living in Ludgvan, who went by the name of 'Yorkshire Jack' (real name Thomas Sampson). Eventually Sarah's love for her new-found sweetheart, and her disgust for her husband, drove her to take drastic action, and her spouse came to an untimely end. The circumstances of his death were deeply suspicious and, although quickly laid to rest, his body was soon dug up for examination. This revealed that old man Polgrean had died of arsenic poisoning, and it would not have taken Agatha Christie to work out that Sarah was the prime suspect. The authorities had little doubt that Sarah had simply snapped and rid herself of her perceived burden, by slipping the poison into his drink. In the coming weeks a trial was arranged and the jury needed little time to pronounce poor Sarah guilty, despite the fact that she had no proper legal defence. The judge then sentenced her to be 'hanged by her neck until dead', only days after her trial (see news extract for details of the full trial – p.102).

LUDGVAN PARISH CHURCH: The gateway leading to the churchyard is reputed to be the main haunt of murderess Sarah Polgrean.

Despite her apparent guilt, the villagers of Ludgvan seemed to take the news of her sentence badly. They all knew how unkindly poor Sarah had been treated by her husband and were deeply opposed to the imminent hanging. Part of the reason for this opposition was the tradition that went back centuries, stating that no child baptised in Ludgvan's Well could be hanged. As Sarah was believed to have been such a child, the superstitious locals feared that having her strung up could only lead to disaster.

However, it was eventually pronounced, after some supposed research into local documents, that Sarah had not after all been baptised there. Ludgvan's residents began to settle down and accept poor Sarah's fate and the forthcoming trial became a major talking point. Whether or not Sarah was baptised in Ludgvan's Well may never be known for sure, although some suggest that the tradition proved to be true, as subsequent events would tell.

On the day of the execution, Sarah was led slowly and purposefully towards the scaffold. There her lover Yorkshire Jack awaited, and he was given permission to accompany her to the platform. The two of them walked hand in hand towards the noose and as the final moments approached, they embraced for the last time. With a last kiss, Sarah was heard to say, 'You will?'

Whatever her assertion, Jack seemed to assent to the request with a simple nod of the head, although many observed that he appeared somewhat reluctant. Nevertheless, Sarah's whole manner altered and despite her impending doom, she became animated and noticeably joyful. Many people wondered what on earth Jack could have agreed to; perhaps there was a plan of rescue. However, it soon became clear that this could not have been on the agenda because Sarah was led forward to have the noose placed around her neck. Her eyes never left Jack and a smile stayed etched upon her face, even as the deadly deed was enacted. Sarah was swiftly despatched to meet her 'Maker' and

1812]	*Ludgvan Marriages.*		123
Henry Thomas, of Crowan, & Mary Roberts		26 Sep.	1808
George Dodge & Jane Prisk, of St. Hilary ...		14 Jan.	1809
Richard Gidley & Bridget Semmons	...	12 Mar.	,,
Henry Richards & Hannah Chelew	...	29 Apr.	,,
William Dunstan & Elizabeth Mitchell	...	27 May	,,
John Murren & Mary Fox	...	12 June	,,
Richard Chelew & Elizabeth Williams	...	18 June	,,
William James & Mary Bell	...	23 July	,,
John Roberts & Jennefer Hicks	...	1 Aug.	,,
Richard Taylor & Ann Curnow ...	...	5 Aug.	,,
John Bawden & Elizabeth Thomas, *lic.*		13 Aug.	,,
George Clements Mitchell, of Lelant, & Julia Martin, *lic.*	...	20 Aug.	,,
John Curnew & Jennifer Stephens, of Zennor		24 Sep.	,,
William Chelew & Ann Hallow ...	...	14 Oct.	,,
John Clements, of St. Erth. & Alice Rowe ...		3 Dec.	,,
John Batten, of Paul, & Jennefer Roberts		17 Dec.	,,
John Gundry & Elizabeth Gidley ...		23 Dec.	,,
Peter Semmens & Jane Martyn, *lic.*	...	20 Jan.	1810
Robert Curnow & Sarah Roach ...	...	1 Feb.	,,
John Hix & Catherine Trewheela, of Madron		26 Mar.	,,
William Thomas, seaman, & Susannah Hooper, w., of North Tawton, co. Devon	...	30 Apr.	,,
Henry Davy Thomas & Ann Catran	...	30 Apr.	,,
John Strick, of Paul, & Mary Lanyon	...	26 Dec.	,,
John Semmens & Elizabeth Hoskin, *lic.*	...	18 Mar.	1811
Thomas Harry & Elizabeth Thomas	...	29 Apr.	,,
Henry Parkin, of Rame, & Mary John, *lic.* ...		28 May	,,
John Penbertthy & Amy Michael ...	...	1 June	,,
Richard Angwin & Elizabeth Lorey	...	23 June	,,
John Kempe & Grace Bottrell	...	13 July	,,
William Roberts, of St. Hilary, & Phillis Mills	...	6 Nov.	,,
Henry Polgreen & Sarah Treman ...	...	9 Nov.	,,
William Mills, of St. Erth, & Ann Trevenen, *lic.*	12 Nov.	,,
Joseph Wearn, of St. Erth, & Thomasin Glasson, *lic.*	...	14 Nov.	,,
James Williams & Elizabeth Warren	...	30 Nov.	,,
William Leggo, w., of Zennor, & Joan Baynard, *lic.* ...	...	6 Jan.	1812

LUDGVAN MARRIAGE REGISTER: This clearly shows the wedding between Sarah and Henry Polgrean (Polgreen) on 9 November 1811.

ROYAL
CORNWALL GAZETTE,
FALMOUTH PACKET & PLYMOUTH JOURNAL.

London Agents,—Messrs. NEWTON and Co. 5, Warwick Square, Newgate Street, and Mrs. WHITE, 33, Fleet Street.

Circulated in CORNWALL, DEVON, DORSET, SOMERSET, and the other WESTERN COUNTIES, and generally throughout the Kingdom.

PRINTED AT Truro, BY T. R. GILLET, JUN.

[No 894.—Price 7d.

...day, August 12, 1820.]

MURDER.

August 10.—The Court was crowded at an early hour this morning, to hear the trial of *Sarah Polgrean*, aged 37, who stood charged with having administered poison to her husband, Henry Polgrean, on the 15th of July last, of which he died on the 18th. The prisoner heard the indictment, and pleaded Not Guilty in a very audible voice. The prisoner having no Counsel, Mr. Williams who was in court, humanely undertook to conduct her defence.

Christopher Ellis Richards had examined the marriage register of the parish of Ludgvan, and found that the prisoner had been married to the deceased, on the 9th of November, 1811.

John Polgrean is brother to the deceased, who was interred on the 20th July last. On the 31st the body was disinterred. He knew it to be his brother's body by the ancles, which were twisted.

W. Trimbath knew the deceased. He was buried in a new piece of ground. Saw the coffin taken up. Knew it was the body of H. Polgrean by his crooked feet.

John Rogers lives at Ludgvan, and knows the prisoner whom he saw at Lelant fair, on the 16th of August last year, selling sweetmeats. She asked him some questions relative to a young man, and said her husband was a jealous hearted old fellow, but she would be up with him in less than twelve months, she would buy two-penny worth of white sugar for him, and that would put him going. Witness said it was hard to put a man going in that way. She said she would do it.

Elizabeth Martin knew the prisoner and the deceased for the last six years. Heard her say she would be d—d if she did not poison the d—d villain. She struck her hand on the table as she spoke; this was in her own house. On the 9th of July last the prisoner, the deceased, and a man named James Tremarthen was at witness's house. The deceased went out, and refused to return, and the prisoner said she should never be rid of the jealous old thing until she had given him a pennyworth. The deceased was buried on the 20th. On the 21st, witness said to prisoner he supposed she would be married again; she replied if she did marry it should be for love, for that she had not loved the deceased more than she loved a dog.—The prisoner here became so much affected that she could not stand, and a chair was ordered for her. As the trial proceeded she fainted several times, and was obliged to be supported.

James Tremarthen knows the prisoner, saw her about two months before the death of her husband, standing near her own door. She said she wished her husband was dead and then she should be married again in three weeks. Witness asked who she would marry; she replied, Thomas Sampson.— Witness said it would be a short courtship. At this time the deceased was about 10 yards from them.— On the 9th of July last, saw her again in company with the deceased and the prisoner at the house of Sarah Martin. The deceased wished the prisoner to go home, and left the house. The prisoner swore he was a jealous old thing, and wished he was dead; but said there no way of putting him going but buying a pennyworth of poison for him.—She was in a great rage when she said this.

Rd. Moyle, jun. surgeon at Penzance, was at Crowlas, in Ludgvan, on the 15th of last month, and stopped at a smith's shop. The deceased came to him and complained of a giddiness in his head and a pain in his stomach. Witness went to his house and bled the deceased; prisoner was present. Witness desired that if the deceased was not better he might hear from him next morning. Prisoner said she had a dose of physic in the house, and asked if she should give it him. Witness understood her to mean a dose of opening medicine, and said she might if he was not better. He did not hear from the deceased next morning and never saw him after alive. On the 31st of last month, the body of the deceased was disinterred. Witness opened the body and took out the stomach,

which he secured, and carried home. The stomach and the contents were examined by witness, and his father. The coat of the stomach was inflamed and in the state that might be expected if the deceased had taken virulent poison. On the inner coat he found some small white particles, which he collected and subjected to a test by mixing them with lamp-black in a glass tube, close at one end. The arsenic was deposited in a crystalline state in the tube after the experiment. He has no doubt it was arsenic in the liquid contents of the stomach, on which he made more than ten experiments, from all of which he found a precipitation of arsenic. He has no doubt the death of the deceased was occasioned by his taking arsenic into his stomach.—He did not believe the deceased had taken what was found in his stomach when witness saw him on Saturday; as if he had, he would have been worse than he then was.

Richard Moyle is father and partner of the last witness, and lives at Marazion. He knew the deceased for many years, and was applied to by Wm. Renowden to send him some medicine, on the 16th of last month. He gave the medicine required, and said he should expect to hear from the deceased next day.—On the 17th the prisoner called on him and told him the sickness had left her husband, who had then only a slight pain in his stomach. Witness gave the same medicine as before. On the 18th, Renowden came again and witness went to Crowlas and saw the deceased who was then dying. He said that all pains had left him; this is always the case with persons poisoned, when mortification takes place. The prisoner asked if he would live three hours; he then left him. He fully agreed in the opinion of his son, as all the experiments were made in his presence, and has no doubt the deceased died of arsenic taken into the stomach. He never was informed by the prisoner that the deceased felt burning and excessive thirst, the grand characteristic symptoms of poison by arsenic.

James Tonkin, a butcher, attends Penzance market. Knows the prisoner. On the 15th July she came to him at Penzance market, and said she was in great trouble about rats which so infested her house, that they ran over them in bed, and that she wanted to poison them, but that Mrs. Harvey would not sell her any poison, as she did not know her. She asked witness to go with her to Mrs. Harvey's to get the poison. Witness said he could not go then, but on her pressing him went, saying she should be careful how she used it, for it was a dangerous thing to meddle with. He told Mrs. Harvey he thought she might let the prisoner have the poison, and it was given to her. The next time he saw the prisoner was on the 27th, when she came to Penzance dressed in black. Witness said Sally what is the matter? she replied "Henry is dead and buried, Honey, since I saw you;—he was ill only three or four days."—Witness exclaimed, "Good God! so sudden."— "Yes," said she, " he is dead and buried."—Witness said, "the rats must have been a token of his death."—The prisoner said, "yes, she supposed they were."—In consequence of what he afterwards heard, he mentioned the prisoner's buying poison at Mrs. Harvey's.

John Harvey druggist at Penzance recollected selling one or two penny worth of arsenic to a woman brought to the shop by last witness on the 15th July. Does not know the prisoner.

Jane Jealous knows the prisoner, and went to her house on the day her husband died. She slept with the prisoner for nine nights after her husband's death. The prisoner told witness that she gave the deceased salts on Sunday morning;—he died on Tuesday. On the 27th, witness told the prisoner Mr. Tonkin said she had bought poison at Penzance and had poisoned the deceased. The prisoner said Mr. Tonkin had never seen her buy any poison. Afterwards she said she had bought a pennyworth of poison at Penzance.— Witness asked why she had bought it, and the prisoner replied, "to poison the rats."—She had never said to witness that the house was infested with rats. Wit-

ness asked whether she had poisoned the rats; and she said she had never used the poison; she had laid it on the shelf of the dresser, and afterwards threw it in the ashes. Sitting up in bed the next morning, when the body was about to be taken up, the prisoner cried out—"Tonkin! Tonkin! What hast thou done to me!—thou hast ruined and undone me."

John Minnet lives at Crowlas. Saw prisoner on the 30th of July, and asked how she could do what she had done. She did not answer for a short time, and then said, she had done no harm to her husband. Witness asked if she had bought the poison. She said, "Yes—but who can testify against me that I gave it him.—Witness asked what she had done with it? Prisoner replied—" There now!"—Witness said she never heard the house was infested with rats. The prisoner answered she had heard rats for two nights on Thursday and Friday, and went to Penzance and bought the poison on Saturday. She brought it home and mixed part of it in dough, and put it in the pantry and locked the door; the rest she left on the dresser; but whether her husband took any of its she could not tell;—he might take it in his tea for sugar; as he was fond of sugar.—Witness asked if she had put any of the poison in the pasty and the prisoner said she had not; that he had fish and butter for dinner on the Saturday (the 15th). Deceased said there was no occasion for butter; but prisoner replied to her husband; " you are poorly, eat a bit of butter."—She said she would not do such a thing (as poison her husband) for a lap full of money; if she could not have agreed with her husband, she would have parted.—The next day the body was taken up, and witness was with the prisoner, who appeared to be in great distress, and clasping her hands cried out; " Oh Tonkin! Tonkin! what hast thou done by me now!—If I am hanged and can come again, I'll tear thee to pieces!"

Frances Renowden lived next door and under the same roof with prisoner for the last ten months. Her house has not been infested with rats, nor did she hear the prisoner complain of them. A clay wall divides the houses, and there is a crack in it, through which rats might pass.

Pearce Rogers, Coroner, searched the prisoner's house, with the Jury that sat on the body, but could find no rat-holes, nor the appearance of any.

Mary Polgrean mother of the deceased, said he was 40 years of age. She saw her son on the Friday before he died, when he did not complain of illness.—Was with him on the Sunday following when he complained of a burning heat inside, and continued to drink cold water. She saw her son on his stomach—He continued to get worse on Monday, and died on Tuesday.

Mr. Moyle, sen. re-called;—said he was surgeon to a club to which the deceased belonged, who was thereby entitled to his advice.—The deceased had not applied for medical assistance before the time he was taken violently ill, nor had the witness seen him for two months before.

The Judge recapitulated the evidence with great precision; and the Jury without hesitation pronounced a verdict of GUILTY.—His Lordship then proceeded to pass the awful sentence of the law, and ordered the prisoner to be executed on Saturday morning, and her body to be given for dissection.—The wretched prisoner, who seemed to be quite insensible, and was obliged to be supported during the time sentence was passing,—she was carried out of the court.

hung limply from the gallows. Over the coming days, Ludgvan was gripped by a fear and panic of unprecedented proportions, as hair-raising stories circulated around the village. People were saying that Sarah's ghost had been walking, and had been clearly observed by several local villagers. Firstly, a man had been heading home from Penzance, at about midnight, past Ludgvan churchyard. Suddenly, he heard the sinister sounds of a spade's heavy thud on the earth, echoing towards him. It seemed that someone was digging in the graveyard. Prompted by the suspicion that grave robbing was afoot, the witness nervously crept into the churchyard to see who was making the noise, and soon wished he had not bothered. There, standing by a headstone, as clear as day, was a white-shrouded figure, highlighted by the moonlight. The figure was of a woman, apparently digging in the grave of the freshly interred Mr Polgrean. As the man stood transfixed with terror observing the scene, the lady turned and looked straight at him. Two cold, sinister eyes pierced his soul and to his horror,

SARAH'S PATH TO THE GRAVE, LUDGVAN CHURCHYARD

POLGREAN FAMILY GRAVE, LUDGVAN CHURCHYARD: Found after an extensive search in the old part of the cemetery by the authors.

he was drawn to witness the ghastly imprints on the figure's neck where livid black lesions, of the sort made only by a rope, stood out on her pale flesh. With one last horrified look, he stared into the eyes of Sarah Polgrean. He had known her well and so sprinted from the gruesome spectacle. Back at his cottage he was visibly seen to shake with fear as he recounted his story.

A few days later, another man was riding along the same road past the churchyard, when his horse became fretful, almost throwing him off. Suddenly he became aware of a white figure heading towards the church. The figure briefly turned and he saw the pale, sickly face of a young woman, a visage of death impressed upon her features. He could also detect the same bruised neck above her white dress. In terror he urged his horse on and galloped quickly away. As he left, he looked at the cemetery once more and saw that the woman had vanished. Nevertheless, he could just make out the sound of digging coming from inside the churchyard walls.

Meanwhile, Yorkshire Jack had begun acting strange. Jack had always been a 'jolly chap' but was now introverted, shunning company, and looking altogether unwell and uncharacteristically nervous. One night he went to Penzance to meet up with a trusty friend and informed him that he had decided to leave and had signed up for service at sea. Apparently, the friend came to learn, this had nothing to do with the death of Sarah, as such. The friend was deeply surprised to hear the real reason though.

Jack told him that he was being haunted by the ghost of Sarah Polgrean. Wherever he went, she was always there and he simply could not evade her. She would appear when he least expected it. The friend was unconvinced and felt that Jack was suffering with his nerves. Still, Jack insisted that he was telling the truth and promised that if the friend stayed long enough by his side, he would be able to prove it. As they began to walk along, the distinct sound of footsteps could be heard behind them. It was clearly the tapping of a woman's heeled shoe and it followed their every step, as they headed back towards Ludgvan. Soon the friend's resolve failed him and he made his excuses, leaving Jack alone with the phantom footsteps. The very next morning Jack left for sea. Immediately, his shipmates noticed strange goings-on. Often Jack would be seen talking to thin air or nervously glancing behind him. Unexplained footsteps were also heard walking on deck, and other strange phenomena were reported. After a few days, Jack confessed to a crew-mate that he believed Sarah's ghost was haunting him, and it was she who was causing all the disturbances. He confided that the day on which he had stood next to Sarah on the scaffold, in front of the hangman's noose, she had begged him to marry her on a certain date, come what may. Hoping to please her in her final moments, Jack had promised that he would, with scant regard for the consequences. Now the 'wedding' date was apparently approaching and he feared he would have to keep his end of the bargain. What this meant he did not know, but he added, 'Tonight shall be my last on this earth.'

Jack was clearly a tormented soul, who genuinely believed that he was being bewitched by Sarah Polgrean's spirit. His troubled mind also believed that she was going to force him to keep his promise. That night, when his ship headed into Mount's Bay, most of the crew were happy to be heading home for a few days, but Jack remained forlorn and subdued.

That evening, as the clock struck twelve, a loud noise could be heard throughout the ship. High-heeled footsteps sounded on deck, clearly moving across the ship, towards Jack's sleeping quarters. He awoke with a look of terrible shock on his face. Fixed in terror, he stepped from his hammock and slowly went up on deck. As he walked, the footsteps could be identified walking alongside him. Then, before anyone could stop him, Jack was seen to hurl himself over the side of the ship into the waters below, and was never seen again. Some even claimed to have seen the form of a young lady briefly appear on deck, moments before Jack toppled overboard. The crew were deeply shocked but there was little they could do. There was even a claim that in an instant, some of them caught the far-away sound of wedding bells peeling out under the water, and a voice they recognised as Jack's was heard declaring, 'I will, I will' over and over again.

LUDGVAN CHURCH GATE TO THE GRAVE-YARD: It was from this point that Sarah Polgrean's ghost was seen to visit her husband's grave.

The Evidence

For centuries after the hanging, people still claimed that Sarah Polgrean haunted Ludgvan's churchyard, and many suggest she still does. It has been advocated that she often appears shrouded in white, with the familiar diabolical black marks on her neck, standing by her husband's tomb. Many believed she was continuously imitating those who exhumed her husband in order to determine his cause of death. Whether Sarah's ghost does still haunt Ludgvan's churchyard cannot be verified, though something strange still seems to occur. Indeed, the churchyard appears to house a sinister white spectre, even today. Recently, various people have claimed independently to witness a frightening apparition in and around the churchyard. The figure is usually observed moving slowly along the road towards the graveyard's entrance, before disappearing through the wall itself.

Others have described a white apparition standing motionless by the graves, only to move off and eventually vanish. This white spectre has also been observed in the gateway of the churchyard. The author has spoken to a person claiming to have seen this figure as recently as the year 2000. This man spotted the terrifying ghost as he was walking past the churchyard late at night. Such sightings can be traced back more than 200 years and it may possibly be a different ghost from that of Sarah Polgrean. Whichever it is, locals will still not venture near the church gates and beyond after nightfall for fear of an encounter.

Others stories have been related by seafarers who claim to have been in Mount's Bay and have heard a strange voice coming from the sea, accompanied by phantom bells, although the exact position is unclear.

Location

Ludgvan can be found just off the A30 between Hayle and Penzance. From Hayle turn right onto the B3309 and just after the village of Crowlas, follow the signs into Ludgvan. Drive through the village in the direction of Castle Gate and Nancledra, until you spot the church and its yard on your right-hand side (SW504331). The church itself is a quaint building with a tower and a typical Cornish village burial site, with fascinating graves bearing local family names.

Also note that nearby is Ludgvan Well (SW502338) where Sarah may or may not have been baptised. This was reputed to have had the power to cure locals of their speech and eye problems. However, its effectiveness was apparently eclipsed when an evil spirit, in anger, spat into the holy healing waters. To visit, take the path directly to the north-west of the church. Follow this through several fields, past a spring on your left and bear right towards a small road. Opposite, on the north-east, is a field where the former healing well is situated.

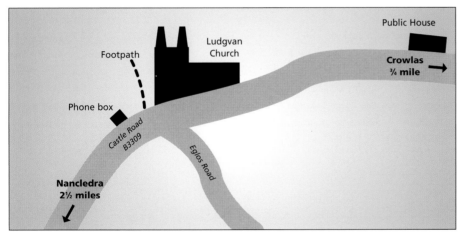

Map, reference to:

Sarah Polgrean, Ludgvan

1815	Mar.31	JOHN SIMMS, A SOLDIER, 30 MURDER OF JOSEPH BURNETT
1818		WILLIAM ROWE, 41 SHEEP STEALING (Not shown on records)
1820	Aug. 12	SARAH POLGREEN, 37 MURDER OF HER HUSBAND
1820	Sept. 5	MICHAEL STEPHENS, 27 KILLING A RAM AND STEALING PART OF CARCASE
1821	April 2	JOHN BARNICOTT, 24 MURDER OF WILLIAM HANCOCK AT CURY
1821	April 2	JOHN THOMPSON, 17 MURDER OF WILLIAM HANCOCK AT CURY
1821	Sept. 10	NICHOLAS JAMES GARD, 42 MURDER OF THOMAS HOSKIN
1825	April 7	WILLIAM OXFORD, 21 SETTING FIRE TO A CORN STACK
1827	April 19	JAMES EDDY, 29 ROBBERY WITH VIOLENCE AND STEALING 7s.
1828	Aug. 8	ELIZABETH COMMONS, 22 MURDER OF HER MALE CHILD
1828	Aug. 21	THOMAS PRING COOMBE, 21 HOUSEBREAKING (2 cases)
1834		WILLIAM HOCKING, 57 BESTIALITY

BODMIN GAOL EXECUTION LIST: All the executions carried out between March 1815 and 1909 are included. Note the range of crimes and the execution of Sarah Polgrean (Polgreen) on 12 August 1820 as seen in this extract taken from the original.

THE GREY LADY, ST MICHAEL'S MOUNT

St Michael's Mount, like Lindisfarne on the north-east coast of England, displays the peculiar quality of being an island and yet also part of the mainland, depending on the movement of the tides. The craggy, tree-covered peak of the Mount carries a monastic fortress dedicated to the patron Saint Michael, whose angelic figure was gloriously observed standing on the highest ramparts of the building or on the rocks some centuries ago. In times past, the towers carried a beacon, which was lit to warn shipping about the reefs in Mount's Bay.

ST MICHAEL'S MOUNT, MARAZION: Home of the legendary giant Cormoran, this island fortress, topped with its magnificent buildings, has many ghost stories, including the Grey Lady. This has been a site of pilgrimage since the fourteenth century.

It seems almost a requisite fact that the ancient granite building, perched today atop the Mount, must have some connection with ghosts and the paranormal. In that respect, the Mount certainly does not disappoint the ghost seeker. The presence of several spirits is well known and reported up until the present day.

The Grey Lady is perhaps the most common spectre and is said to haunt the long passage area of the castle. She is believed to be the ghost of a maid-servant who once worked for the St Aubyn family. Her wraith has been witnessed on numerous occasions, each time by visitors, staff and the resident family.

Her tale is of a tragic love affair with one of the sons of the residing lord many years ago. It was said that she bore his child and, despite her inferior social position, a wedding was swiftly arranged. However, the groom is said to have rejected his young bride, jilting her at the altar. She immediately fled from the monastery chapel and entered the long passage. There she climbed a wall at its end and stepped on to the battlements. With a broken heart, she threw herself over the edge, falling to her death on the rocks, hundreds of feet below.

There is also said to be an amusing phantom, which likes to turn doorknobs throughout the building with an unseen, spectral hand. He or she also enjoys hiding objects in different locations, only to reveal them some days later. The identity of this prankster is unknown, but a monk, presumably representing a throw back to the days of the monastery, is also believed to haunt an area near the chapel. There is also an old bed in the castle itself, in which few are able to sleep undisturbed.

Finally, the chapel may be haunted by another ghostly figure and this para-normal activity seemed to increase some years ago after the bones of a 17½-foot giant were unearthed in a crypt under the chapel's floor. Whether or not these were remains of the giant Cormoran, who legend claims built and lived on the Mount, is anybody's guess.

The Evidence

The Grey Lady has succeeded in providing staff, family and visitors with a strong tally of appearances, often disappearing quickly at the end of the passage. Often she is heard but not seen, walking in the long passage, the loose tiles under the carpet echoing to her footfalls, even when no living person is in that part of the building. Two members of a well-known paranormal research group visited recently and recorded some cold spots in the long passage, accompanied by a strong feeling of 'weight' on their shoulders and a depressive atmosphere.

The playful poltergeist which turns door handles and moves objects has been sensed on many occasions; doors have also opened by themselves or started rattling for no apparent reason. The ghost is believed to be friendly and is in no way threatening or malicious. Its trick of cunningly hiding household objects in the most unlikely of places is considered mischievous, rather than malevolent.

Visitors to the monastic castle fortress have often stated that they have noticed a distinct drop in temperature in certain areas, particularly the long passage. The latter and the chapel also evoke a feeling of depression and melancholy to the unwary. This would seem to tie up with the Grey Lady's sad misfortunes.

Location

St Michael's Mount (SW514298) can usually be seen well before it is reached. It is situated near the village of Marazion and is accessible on foot from here for a period of several hours daily, on each side of low tide (consult a local book of tide times for accuracy). At high tide, visitors may use the regular motor launches, at a small charge, to cross the sea. Admission to the monastery is via the National Trust site and the walk uphill is arduous and not advisable for the elderly or those with particular health problems. Once at the top, the building is well worth a visit and the views from the battlements on a clear day are spectacular. Marazion is now bypassed by the A394 Penzance to Helston road. If you have travelled from these directions, you will need to leave the A394 and head into Marazion, following the signs. Drive through the narrow streets. You can either park at the Red River and sand dunes

(SW507312) or at one of the small car parks facing the Mount (space permitting in season), above the beach (SW513310).

THE MERMAID OF LAMORNA, LAMORNA COVE

There is a well-known mermaid story, centred on a location less than 7 miles from Zennor. The attractive young mermaid of this tale was said to have frequented her resting place on the top of Half Tide Rock, to the north-eastern side of Lamorna Cove, over many years. Her presence was not a good omen for passing sailing ships, since, as she sang her mournful, heart-rending songs, a shipwreck would inevitably follow somewhere close to the cove. Locally, it was claimed that the melancholy chanting could be heard accompanied by the sound of other terrestrial spirits, and this sad sound was very disturbing for

LAMORNA COVE: Half Tide Rock, where the mermaid is said to sit and sing, can be seen at the end of the cliff line.

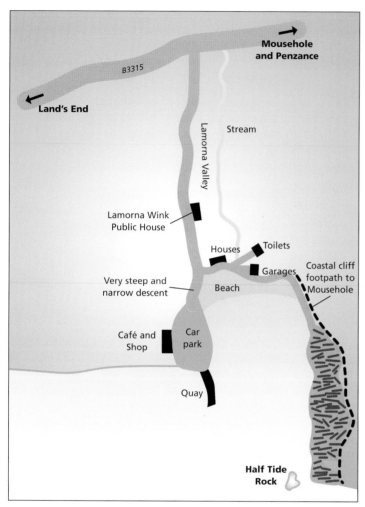

Map, *reference to:*

The Mermaid of Lamorna

those who heard it. However, like the Sirens told of by the Greek poet Homer, when the songs were at their most enchanting, young Lamorna men, if unwary, could be lured out into the sea and when they tried to reach the mermaid's rock, they would never be seen again.

The Evidence

The sound of the restless waves ceaselessly breaking on the Lamorna harbour entrance may have given credence to the music of the deep. As far as the authors are aware, there has been no definitive record of the mermaid's song for some years, and certainly no sightings of her either. Nevertheless, Cornwall seemed to abound with these stories of lovely young maidens of the deep. During previous centuries, there are records pertaining to the resident mermaids at many locations, including: Lamorna, Zennor, Padstow, Perranporth and the Lizard.

Location

Lamorna Cove is about a mile off the B3315 from Newlyn and Penzance. The route is served by bus at most times of the year and the wooded Lamorna Valley offers the visitor a taste of a sylvan extravaganza after leaving the main route across the coast. Lamorna Cove has very limited parking space, a small beach, depending on the state of the tide, and some outstanding cliff scenery, if viewed from the cliff-top paths. Refreshments are available in season at a small café. Half Tide or Mermaid Rock is visible, depending on the tide, below the cliff path from Mousehole. It is situated on the north of Lamorna Cove, about half a mile from the quay (SW455239).

LUTEY AND THE MERMAID, BEREPPER SANDS

Another of the mysterious mermaid legends concerns a young man named Lutey, hailing from the hamlet of Cury. Perhaps not surprisingly, a good number of such stories have a highly romantic theme, involving, as they invariably do, handsome young men who become irresistibly entangled with these beautiful aquatic creatures.

In just such a manner, young Lutey was walking on Berepper Beach one summer's evening, when he met a lovely mermaid marooned by the outgoing tide and weeping fitfully. Being a God-fearing, family man, Lutey carried the mermaid gently back to the edge of the sea. Here Morvena, as the mermaid was called, offered him a golden comb and a promise of her future guidance in all difficulties. She told Lutey that he would be able to summon her at any time by combing his hair three times and calling her name. Lutey was also granted three wishes. These he decided would be: protection from witchcraft; an ability to control spirits, in order to assist the needy; and lastly to keep these powers in his family forever.

As in the 'Mermaid of Zennor' tale, Morvena tried to entice her new-found hero back to the deep as her husband, but Lutey was having none of it. She therefore gave him nine years of freedom before she would return to claim Lutey for herself. Lutey was allowed to prosper, in time becoming a famous local white wizard, gaining the power to heal the sick and aid the unfortunate. However, he also soon forgot the terms of his 'parole'.

Exactly nine years later, whilst he was fishing in his boat off the Loe Bar with a friend, Morvena returned. She surfaced in the calm of the evening tide and called for Lutey to come. With a little hesitation, Lutey accepted his summons and leapt overboard to join his mermaid. His body was never recovered and he was never seen again. It was left to Lutey's friend to break the news of this dramatic departure to Lutey's family.

The Evidence

All of the mermaid legends do have some basis in fact and all of them have ingredients of similar ilk. The promise is of wonderment beneath the waves, to be exchanged for human existence. Although the only witness at the time was Lutey's friend, some credence must be given to the fact that several white witches and benevolent healers descended from Lutey's family and lived locally.

Location

The small village of Cury (SW678213) can be reached from the A3083 Lizard to Helston road along the small lane to Poldhu Cove. It was here on the head-land, that Marconi broadcast the first transatlantic Morse wireless message at

LOE BAR AND BEREPPER SANDS: The full extent of Loe Bar is visible from the left-centre of the photograph. Berepper Sands stretch from the centre ground to the distant right.

the beginning of the twentieth century. The scenery along the Lizard is typically rocky, with sheer cliffs and tiny coves. Berepper Sands, where the mermaid was first found, stretch from Loe Bar (SW643242) to Gunwalloe Cove (SW654225).

THE MERMAID OF ZENNOR

Vear Cove, Zennor, is the source of one of Penwith's most unusual and famous legends. It features the Mermaid of Zennor, described as a fine, beautiful woman with long golden tresses, seaweed-green eyes and wearing an elegant, shimmering, long silver-coloured dress. She made her appearance one Sunday summer morning at the granite village church of Zennor, situated on the north side of the Penwith peninsula and close to the resort of St Ives.

She entered the church quietly as the service began and sat alongside the entrance door, well apart from the congregation. Many eyes turned to view this exquisite newcomer but, in return, the mermaid fixed her gaze on Matthew Trewella, a handsome young tenor sitting in the church choir. At the end of the lengthy service, the mermaid left as quietly as she had entered and was seen heading in the direction of the cliffs. She had spoken to no one and had departed too hastily for Matthew to introduce himself. This beautiful creature returned Sunday after Sunday, obviously bewitched by Matthew and his singing. Each week, as the vicar concluded the service with a final blessing, she had already vanished from the building.

Then one Sunday in late autumn, Matthew made the decision that he must meet this mysterious woman and left the choir stalls early, before the blessing. He followed his unknown admirer towards the sea cliffs and as he reached a small stream, which still flows into Pendour Cove over the cliffs, she quickly turned. They spoke for a few minutes and then the mermaid, grabbing Matthew's arm, led him along the cliffs to Vear Cove Beach. Entering the sea, they were both quickly submerged by the waves. Matthew never returned home, but some years later a passing ship anchored in the cove to draw fresh water from the stream and collect supplies from the neighbouring farms. A party of the ship's crew rowed ashore in a long boat, whilst the captain remained on board. Later, on watch, he suddenly heard a woman's sweet voice cry out, 'Captain, will you haul up your anchor for 'tis blocking the door of my cave. I can't get inside to Matthew and our children.' The startled seaman peered down over the ship's rail and saw a green-eyed mermaid with long golden hair. 'Did you say Matthew?' he asked. 'Yes,' she responded, 'now haul up your anchor please.' The captain hurriedly raised the anchor, just as the mermaid vanished under the water.

The story became so well known in the Zennor locality that the lovely mermaid was captured for all time in a carving on a wooden bench-end situated towards the front of the Zennor church, in an old side chapel. Also of interest to the visitor is the leper-squint window through the interior nave wall. This offered lepers, deemed unclean, the opportunity to watch the service from a side chapel without mixing with the congregation.

The Evidence

Many local people claim to have seen a mermaid around the Zennor area, though it is usually a seal swimming through the waves. Indeed, traditionally in other parts of the world, the sea cow has been the real-life creature thought to give rise to mermaid folklore. Whether or not any sightings are genuine is difficult to substantiate. Certainly though, there are some interesting aspects to this particular story which might bear consideration for the avid paranormal investigator, before he or she dismisses the account as pure folk legend.

Firstly, Trewella, Matthew's surname, is indeed a genuine Cornish name, for there are still a considerable number of locals in West Penwith bearing this title. Whether any can claim to be a direct ancestor of the union of Matthew and the mermaid may be more debatable.

THE MERMAID BENCH-END, ZENNOR CHURCH: This ancient carving clearly shows the mermaid of the story.

Secondly, the story is so unusual that surely there must be at least some element of truth; 'no smoke without fire'. The sequence of events, including the appearance of a female stranger and Matthew's disappearance, does perhaps ring true.

Thirdly, Vear Cove is a deep anchorage and will certainly hold a large sailing vessel, whilst, of course, there is a freshwater stream for liquid supplies.

Finally, there have been numerous occasions over the past centuries when visitors have claimed to hear enchanted music and melodious voices borne on the wind. These seemingly rise from Vear Cove and the choral refrain has apparently been heard until recent times. Who may be responsible for such alluring song is not known, but of course Matthew, a famed member of the local choir, and a mermaid would certainly be able to put one or two notes together!

The Location

Zennor church and village can be approached from either St Ives or St Just on the B3306. This is a winding road and can be dangerous, owing to the amount of traffic at certain times, such as the summer months, and as a result of the constant twists and turns of the route – the edges of the road are often boulder-strewn and unforgiving to any misjudgements in steering. Nevertheless, the views are without doubt some of the most outstanding seascapes in the whole of Cornwall. On a clear summer's day, with a golden sun, the spirits of the beholder of such breathtaking scenery cannot fail to be uplifted by the natural panorama.

Zennor church (SW454386) is certainly worth a visit, the village and church being just a few hundred yards from the road. There is limited parking by the church, at the Tinner's Arms pub and in the nearby village car park. As previously mentioned, the church houses the fifteenth-century mermaid bench-end depicting the heroine of our tale, with her long hair, mirror and comb (see illustration opposite).

For the more adventurous explorer, take the narrow lane behind the Tinner's Arms and walk towards the sea. After about half a mile, leave the tarmac road and walk downhill by the steps across the stream, above Pendour Cove (SW448389), and follow in the wake of Matthew and his beloved mermaid bride, to the adjacent and unusually sandy Vear Cove (SW445388).

Map, reference to:

1 The Mermaid of Zennor
2 The Seaman's Ghost of Zennor

NB: The Tinner's Arms provides excellent food and ale, particularly during the tourist season.

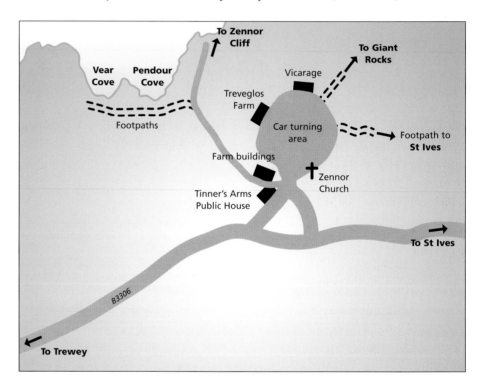

MADGE FIGGY, WITCH AND WRECKER, LAND'S END

This story is well-steeped in the supernatural and involves the world of witch-craft, of which Cornwall can boast several famous examples: The Witch of Trewey, Zennor; Harry the Thief at Tol-Pedn-Penwith and Betty Trenoweth of St Buryan, to name but a few.

Madge Figgy was a 'black witch' who became the leader of the fearsome St Levan witches and a gang of Cornish wreckers. They supposedly lured passing sailing ships on to rocks around Porthcurno and Porthgwarra. For Madge and her band, using lanterns tied to several donkeys on the cliffs, as is often assumed, was not enough; they were also prepared to conjure up storms. Madge used to sit on her cliff rock perch at the 'Chair Ladder', west of Porthgwarra Cove, and use terrifying spells to raise a tempest at sea. This channel, from Land's End and eastwards, is well known for its sudden squalls, which can change the sea from a flat, windless blue landscape to an ashen-grey rolling torment in the space of a few hours. It is easy to see how, in past centuries, people could believe such turbulent weather to be influenced by witchcraft. Today's scientific explanations of a rapidly deepening, eastward-flowing collapse of air pressure would have meant nothing to those living there hundreds of years before.

One interesting tale of Madge's exploits refers to a Portuguese merchant ship, laden with jewels, fine clothes and treasure. Madge made sure that the ship would be wrecked and that all the corpses would wash into the local bay, where they could be stripped of valuables. Nevertheless, one finely dressed woman was left alone. It was said that she bore a special mark, which signified death to anyone who stole from her. Madge ordered that the woman be buried but that her goods should be stored in a chest at her own cottage. Over the next three nights, strange lights were witnessed issuing from the woman's grave on the cliffs. These lights were said to stop at the Chair Ladder where Madge Figgy had sat to lure ships to their destruction.

TOL-PEDN-PENWITH, PORTHGWARRA: The lofty site of Madge Figgy's Chair Ladder, overlooking the unpredictable Atlantic Ocean. This is where she is said to have carried out her despicable deeds of witch-craft and wrecking.

A dark stranger soon entered St Levan and asked for the whereabouts of any graves belonging to those drowned from the Portuguese ship. At the grave of the woman, the stranger showed extreme grief. He was then led to Madge Figgy's cottage by the peculiar lights, which had been seen on several previous nights. The stranger helped himself to all of the jewellery and clothes from the chest, giving the witch and her gang some rich rewards for their assumed honesty. Later the stranger revealed that he was also a black witch, capable of cursing the whole group to an instant death. If Madge had decided to steal the treasure for herself, it might have been the last evil deed she would have performed.

The Evidence

Local memories of Madge and her feared gang have long disappeared, although witchcraft, both black and white, still exists in various forms throughout the South West. Whilst the activities of Madge and her fellow evil wreckers have been relegated to the annals of folklore, shipwrecks still occur with alarming regularity around the Cornish coast. The winter of 2002 witnessed several large wrecks in the area and some locals were still happy to remove any cargo which fortuitously arrived on their beaches. The hamlet of Raftra (SW376233), where Madge Figgy's cottage stood, still survives, as does the Chair Ladder seat where she was said to organise shipwrecks. (This can be visited beneath the coast-guard lookout station, west of Porthgwarra Cove.) Some people claim that even today, on a dark, windswept night, cries can be heard sweeping in from Madge Figgy's chair. The sound is of Madge cackling to herself still, about the misery she caused and the poor souls who perished as a result of her greed and black magic.

Location

By following the same directions quoted for the 'William and Nancy' story, to Porthgwarra, one finds oneself near the Chair Ladder location. Use the large car park and walk on to Hella Point, taking the lower path along the cliff edge to the Chair Ladder. This lies beyond the coastguard station on the cliff top (SW365216). The walk can be very dangerous, being at certain points right on the edge of the cliff. However, sea views here are dramatic and awe-inspiring at any time of the year. Be careful during offshore gales on any cliff paths, since fatalities are still all too common in any season among unwary visitors (map p.73).

Mysterious Cries and Strange Phenomena

The Hooper – Sennen Cove
Screams at Battery Rocks – Penzance
The Phantom Revellers – Mount's Bay
The Captain's Tomb – St Levan
Jack Harry's Lights – Cornish Coast
The Lost Lands of Lyonesse – Mount's Bay
Demon Tregeagle – Loe Bar, Porthcurno

THE HOOPER, SENNEN COVE

Cornwall's south-west peninsula is almost overflowing with environmental spirits who are said to dwell in trees, wells, streams and, of course, on the coastline. One of the strangest legends is of the unusual 'Spirit Guardian' of the sea at Sennen Cove, known as 'The Hooper'.

On the north-west edge of Sennen Cove, just beyond the present lifeboat station, is a rocky reef, which at times of storm provides spectacular plumes of sea spray and a melodrama of sound. This reef, known as the Cowloe Rocks, has been responsible for several terrible shipwrecks, and the channel between the coast and the reef, known as The Tribbens, is narrow and risky at any state of the tide.

The Land's End peninsula at certain times of the year can be affected by dense sea fogs, which roll in without warning from far out at sea. The proximity of the coast, the constantly changing atmospheric conditions, the temperature differences between land and sea and the unpredictable, unstable air currents in this small area, can clothe the whole district with swirling, dense white mists which seem to deaden all sounds with eerie stillness.

The Hooper usually begins to form over the Cowloe Rocks, quickly spreading across the whole of Sennen's bay like a white wall of smoke. The manifestation is said to emit a dull glow at night from the middle of the fog-bank, along with showers of rising sparks. Locals believed that the fog was a mantle for the spirit of the sea and could be heard to produce whooping noises, adding to the fear caused to anyone around Whitesand Bay.

The Hooper's appearance has been recorded over past centuries and still occasionally in the present day. The strange spectral mist dampens a clear and empty bay, appearing from nowhere and entombing the whole landscape. Its purpose stands as a warning before the arrival of vicious storms from the sea. Folklore records that the names of drowned sailors can often be heard above the howling wind as the tempest reaches the land.

The Evidence

The presence of The Hooper is a longstanding and widely acknowledged fact at Whitesand Bay, although the mists today rarely seem to carry the frightening cries, ethereal lights and sparks, which were noted with terror during past centuries. Many locals and visitors still give testimony to the sudden arrival of the fog-banks in Whitesand Bay. Who can be sure that, in the ferocity of the approaching storm, the spine-chilling cries of drowned seamen are in reality only the screams of the whirling seabirds, and not the spirits of the dead looking for shelter ashore?

Location

Sennen Cove and Whitesand Bay are reached just before Land's End by leaving the A30 about 1½ miles after the junction with the B3306 to St Just. The descent to Sennen Cove is very steep and the car parking is limited at the sea

COWLOE REEF, TRIBBENS CHANNEL, SENNEN: Photographed from the North Pier car park, Sennen Cove. Cape Cornwall appears across Whitesand Bay, top right.

front. The Cowloe Rocks are on the north edge of the bay (SW349267) and there is a small car park beside the jetty, overlooking the point and the rocks. From a position beside the lifeboat station, the magnificent view of Whitesand Bay can be appreciated, when looking across the sea to the east.

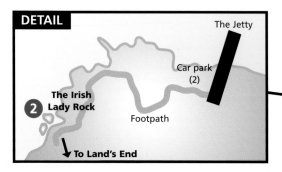

Map, reference to:

1 The Hooper (see p.122)
2 The Irish Lady (see p.98)
3 The First and Last Inn (see p.51)

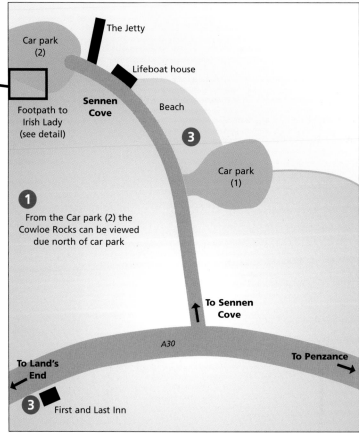

SCREAMS AT BATTERY ROCKS, PENZANCE

The area known as Battery Rocks in Penzance has both an intriguing history and a sinister reputation. The rocks are no strangers to death, and after dark can take on an eerie appearance, as well as being the site of an extremely strange phenomenon, which has yet to be explained.

They also play a pivotal part in Penzance's history. When the original name 'Pensans' first appeared on the map in 1284, the town was little more than a tiny fishing settlement perched by the sea. This settlement grew into the thriving town of today, but at the time was situated around Battery Rocks. In 1739 the 'battery' itself was erected here in preparation for yet another possible war with Spain and ongoing hostilities with France. It was heavily armed during both the First and Second World Wars and many of its fortifications lie

BATTERY ROCKS, PENZANCE: This rocky outcrop is no stranger to tragedy and it is here that terrifying screams are said to be heard.

underneath the present-day outdoor bathing pool. Today the war memorial stands proudly by the rocks' edge and the 'art deco' bathing pool sits adjacent to the promontory.

The rocks themselves are now almost synonymous with tragedy. Over the centuries copious numbers of people have died at this small yet merciless spot. Many, too, have drowned nearby, their limp and lifeless bodies later thrown up on to the rocks. However, the statistics never elucidate the personal tragedies each death brings. For example, a young man's body was discovered here just last year after drowning in the sea, his promising life cut tragically short, and he was certainly not the first.

People have also died here in other ways; many are unable to resist the temptation to dive into what can be calm and blue waters, unaware of the number of hidden boulders lying under the waves. It was said that Penzance's most famous 'son', Sir Humphry Davy, enjoyed doing so, although he seemed to possess an uncanny awareness of the rocks' positions; perhaps just as well for the sake of chemistry and mining alike.

Many others have been either not so astute or less fortunate. Over forty years ago a young man perished here after he ventured on to the granite outcrops late at night. He had drunk a large amount of alcohol and was discovered the next morning, cold and lifeless in a pool of blood on the rocks. It was presumed that he had lost his footing in his drunken state and had cracked his skull open on the hard surface.

Such accounts of tragedy give rise to a healthy respect for one's surroundings, but also may be a prerequisite for stories of the supernatural. It can be assumed that those aware of past events may be predestined to experience grief or sadness when visiting this grim place. However, many are not prepared for the emotions, which can overtake them. It is common for people to be standing, overlooking the rocks, and to feel suddenly a deep sense of unease and fearful anticipation. This feeling often comes before a spine-chilling sound, strong enough to strike terror into the hardiest of ghost hunters. An earth-shattering shriek or scream suddenly arises, coming from the rocks themselves. The noise is brief yet is unmistakably of human origin, as if somebody is in desperate need of assistance. Many people have been so concerned that they have immediately rushed down on to the rocks to search for the source of the sound and the person in distress. But their investigations prove to be fruitless, as they discover just empty rocks, with absolutely nothing unusual to be seen.

The Evidence

The abundance of people who have claimed to hear these terrible cries is truly extraordinary, particularly on windy or stormy nights. People have, of course, attempted to explain the sounds through rational means. Suggestions include: a howling wind, gulls flying overhead, a crying seal, a dolphin (very unlikely this close to land), and others. In some ways a few of these explanations may ring true. However, many of the people who have heard the noises first hand have been insistent that the 'scream' was convincingly a person in torment, and many of them should be taken seriously because they are fully aware of the types of noises heard in and around the sea.

There may yet be a perfectly natural reason for such screams to be heard. Perhaps, though, as many have suggested, the noises are related to the death and tragedy in this area. Maybe some lost soul is crying out in panic as they might have done just before their untimely death, or perhaps a past event has been imprinted on the granite crags, to be unleashed at certain times to unsuspecting passers-by.

Location

Battery Rocks lie just around the corner from Penzance's harbour and just before the start of the promenade (SW478297). Drive into Penzance on the A30 and follow the road past the railway station. Get into the left-hand lane and follow the road over Ross Bridge, carry on past the harbour on the left. Just around the corner is the path to the rocks, on the left-hand side. There is limited parking by the bay, marked areas on the side of the road and a car park slightly further on, on the right. The path leads down to the left of the bathing pool and loops around to the back of the pool. From this position one can gaze at some magnificent views of the bay and St Michael's Mount. At certain times of the year you may also be lucky enough to spot the odd seal, which may occasionally venture into the area. One could also take a short stroll to Penzance's harbour and several other locations described in this book (map p.43).

(The photograph of Chimney Rocks earlier in this book also shows Battery Rocks in part. They are just off the swimming pool and the Mount is in the bay beyond – see p.40.)

THE PHANTOM REVELLERS, MOUNT'S BAY

In Mount's Bay there is an account referring to ghostly voices being heard, linked to the following tale. Long ago, one of the many rich lords of Pengersick (Praa Sands, SW579283) was a prosperous landowner who loved nothing better than to show off his vast fortune. One fine summer's day he could not resist taking out a group of acquaintances aboard a large boat for an afternoon's jaunt around Mount's Bay. The party spent the day feasting and over-indulging themselves to the utmost degree.

Suddenly, as the end of the day approached, the boat overturned and sank in the calm waters. There seemed to be no explanation as to why disaster should have struck the ill-fated passengers, without warning, although many suspected that drunken tomfoolery was the likely culprit. It is believed that on calm days out in the bay the ill-fated group can still be heard drifting across the still waters, singing and crying out as if part of some eternal revelry.

The Evidence

Unfortunately, the authors have not been able to trace any witnesses to the sounds. In reality, it is very likely that this story is one of the tales associated with Pengersick Castle, which bears little relation to fact and is more likely just a legend.

Location

Although the noises are claimed to be heard in the area of Mount's Bay, the exact location of the sounds is unknown. Nevertheless, if you should go for an enjoyable boat trip out in the bay and happen to hear strange voices drifting across the water, please do let the authors know, and please take note of your exact position!

THE CAPTAIN'S TOMB, ST LEVAN

A short distance west of Porthcurno (SW388222) is the sheltered and pretty little church of St Levan, the focus for a saga of shipwreck and ghostly bells. The original plan was for the church to be constructed at nearby Raftra at the head of the valley. However, it seems that supernatural forces had other plans and each night the building materials were transported away. The next day these had been deposited at the present location, situated at the end of a small and narrow cul-de-sac road.

The strange account unfolds that in December 1811, the sailing brig *Aurora,* captained by Richard Wetherall, sprang a serious leak in heavy weather and sank near the Runnel Stone off Land's End. The crew escaped in a rowing boat but the captain refused to leave his ship and was drowned. He was

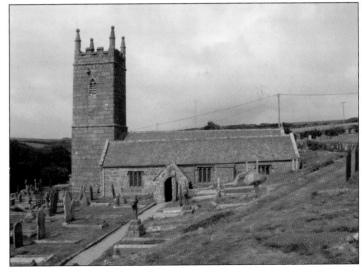

ST LEVAN CHURCH: *This lonely and picturesque site is the location for Captain Richard Wetherall's tomb and the phantom bell.*

buried in this remote churchyard but his grave is said to still hold a very disturbing warning.

It is said that the captain had insisted on remaining on the sinking ship until the very end, and just before the ship disappeared under the waves, he sounded out a last desperate ring of eight foreboding bells. This was to signal the end and soon he began his journey to the seabed.

For many years, it has been suggested that the Captain's last resting place was regarded with fear and wonder since it is claimed that a ghostly bell will strike at full or half-hours, below the surface of the grave. Apparently the bell will peel particularly loudly at midday and midnight, and is far more audible when the full eight bells chime out their mournful cacophony. Unfortunately though, since the eight bells are said to signal the end of the *Aurora*, to hear the phantom sounds is said to foretell disaster, namely the death of the listener.

The Evidence

One Sunday afternoon years ago, several young people were visiting St Levan churchyard after the morning service had started. The youths decided to stay outside in the pleasant sunshine and not to follow their parents inside the church. They were rambling among the graves when one young girl came by chance upon the tomb of Captain Wetherall, and read the inscription. Without warning, from below her feet, suddenly sounded the sombre, hollow tolling of a bell. The others heard it as well and the group swiftly fled into the church, out of sheer terror. The time was precisely midday. The story became well known in the village and a few weeks later, a young local returned home from sea to hear the tale related in the village pub. He scoffed that it was nonsense and boasted of his plans to visit the graveside to prove it. He thus took some friends and ventured into the churchyard just as midday approached. Whilst his companions waited in the church porch and observed their friend, they all watched the sundial as the shadow moved up to the mark of noon. The sailor was standing by the Captain's gravestone. At precisely midday, he was seen

MAIN PORCH, ST LEVAN CHURCH: Note the sundial over the Norman archway, featured in the story of Richard Wetherall's grave.

fleeing back to his companions and pronouncing, ''Tis true as I'm alive; I heard the eight bells struck beneath his grave and I wouldn't go back near the spot again for the world.' On the sailor's next voyage, the experienced young mariner met his untimely death by drowning.

According to local residents, the bells have been heard right up to recent times, tolling mournfully beneath the earth. Whether or not the death of the witness follows is not noted.

Location

From Porthcurno car park (SW384225) off the B3315 (the turn between Treen and Little Trethewey), take the narrow, uphill winding lane past the famous Minack Theatre and continue, passing several properties, for about half a mile, to reach St Levan church (SW381223). You may park in the field just to the right, before the churchyard. This also gives access on foot to the rugged and inspiring Porth Chapel Beach, which continually bears the brunt of the wild Atlantic Ocean. Above the beach is the famous St Levan hermitage and holy well, the waters of which are said to cure toothache!

For interest, before you leave St Levan graveyard, find the large split granite boulder, quite near the porch. This was supposedly halved by St Selevan himself, who, at the time, prophesied, 'When with panniers astride, a packhorse can ride through St Levan's stone, the world will be done.'

Thus, it might be advisable to check that the gap is still just wide enough to allow you to squeeze through before you depart. If there is enough room for a horse, with baskets either side (if you happen to have one available, complete with panniers!) then it might be that the end of the world is nigh!

Map, reference to:

The Captain's Tomb, St Levan

1 *Khyber* Grave
2 St Selevan Cleft Boulder
3 The Sundial (over the porch)
4 The Phantom Ship of Porthcurno

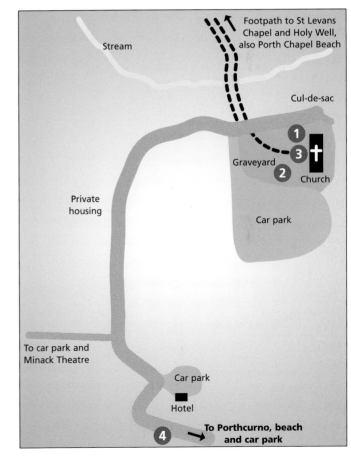

The churchyard to the left of the entrance porch also contains the mass grave and plaque to the memory of the drowned victims of the sailing ship *Khyber*, lost 15 March 1905 at Land's End. At least 23 unfortunates died in this terrible tragedy and some of their remains are buried in this peaceful and beautiful churchyard location.

Above: *ST SELEVAN'S CLEFT ROCK, ST LEVAN CHURCHYARD: Co-author Ian nervously considers whether his loaded packhorse will fit through the gap.*

Above right: KHYBER *PLAQUE, ST LEVAN CHURCHYARD: A mass grave to the memory of those who perished in the wreck of the* Khyber *at nearby Porthloe Cove, in the dreadful storm of March 1905.*

JACK HARRY'S LIGHTS, CORNISH COAST

Strange lights are a persistent phenomenon across the world. Whether such things can be explained by ball lightning, U.F.O.s, natural phenomena, earth energy, fairies or even perhaps Father Christmas's elves is debatable. However, unexplained light phenomena undoubtedly do exist. In particular, Cornwall (especially around the Land's End peninsula) seems to be uncannily linked to mysterious lights, which have been recorded for centuries. These have led to a great deal of folklore and legend, yet they are still seen persistently across the Cornish land and seascapes.

Peculiar lights in Cornwall have traditionally been attributed to the fairy folk. It was believed, for example, that the mischievous piskies often appear with a welcoming light for people to follow, beckoning them on towards a bog or other unfortunate circumstance. On moorland and at ancient stone sites, numerous people have claimed to see multi-coloured lights dancing across the countryside. This was believed to have represented the fairy folk lighting up their surroundings for their nocturnal revelry. The lights are also said to predict a forthcoming disaster, especially when they often appeared in mines. Locals claimed that these were created by candle-bearing spirits of long-dead miners, warning their fellow 'brethren'. Indeed there are countless references to all kinds of strange lights across the county: balls of light rolling across the ground, lights dancing on the cliff tops, blue lights darting inside buildings, mysterious glows emanating from churches and graveyards, luminous yellow flames rising from the ground, peculiar orbs, and many other examples.

Particularly in West Cornwall, many of these strange lights are known as 'Jack Harry's Lanterns'. These are believed by many to be spectral lights, perhaps the souls of long-dead sailors or of other spirit origin. Again they are said to often herald disaster, such as an impending storm or perhaps a lost vessel. Sometimes it is claimed that they also appear on a ship, forewarning of its approaching fate. Suggestions are that these lights may be accompanied with phantom vessels.

In reality there may be many explanations for strange lights: the aforementioned ball lightning, unknown earth energies or other natural phenomenon. A likely contender is the will-o'-the-wisp, phosphorescent light seen on marshy ground, believed to be ignited gas, or perhaps a chemical reaction. Certainly these lights are often seen around boggy ground. Geological factors may be important: tectonic stress on fault lines and so-called 'earthquake lights'. A more recent explanation gaining worldwide recognition is the theory about 'orbs', which have been captured on numerous films (including by the authors), particularly at 'haunted' locations. These lights can vary in size and shape (though usually spherical) and seem to move intelligently, sometimes interacting with objects or people. They seem to travel independently and are difficult to explain in rational terms. Increasing numbers believe these to be the energy which remains after death; in essence, the soul. Indeed many orbs do contain quite elaborate patterns and even facial structures. Many researchers are spending a great deal of time attempting to link these orbs with ghosts and spirit activity.

It is a fascinating area and yet familiar. Theories linking strange balls of light to lost souls are not such a recent phenomenon. Indeed the Cornish have been talking about Jack Harry's Lights for centuries, and to many of them, they would never dream that they could be anything else other than the visible presence of the undead.

The Evidence

Sightings of lights seem to be just as frequent up to the present day. They have been recorded for many centuries and in all cultures across the world, yet they are perhaps still as mysterious as in the past. Whether they are truly spirits of ancient people, fairy folk or a long-occurring natural phenomenon has not been established, but you do stand a good chance of seeing or photographing such 'paranormal' activity in Cornwall.

Location

Strange lights are seen in a vast array of places around Cornwall, and in particular, marshland, cemeteries, haunted buildings, moorland, cliff paths, and especially near cromlechs. These burial stones may be your best chance of being a witness, especially during storms, though do be careful! Particular 'hotspots' include:

Carn Kenidjack and surrounding moor (SW388329).
Take the A3071 to St Just, continue along Fore St, turning left into Cape Cornwall Street. Then move right into Chapel Road, up Nancherrow Hill and

right into No Go By Hill. Walk down 'Water Lane' on to Carnyorth Common, following the footpath past Carn Kenidjack and on to the moor.

Logan Rock (SW397220).
Follow the A30 Penzance to Land's End road through Drift and Catchall, turning left onto the B3283 to Treen. Follow the signs to Logan Rock and the car park at the end of the cul-de-sac.

Ballowal Barrow (Carn Gluze/Gloose) (SW356313).
Follow the A3071 Penzance to St Just road into St Just and onwards into Fore Street. At the square turn left into Cape Cornwall Street and keep to this road until you reach Cape Cornwall Road; move on past the cricket ground (to your right). Turn left into Carn Gloose road and follow this for less than a mile. Ballowal Barrow is on the cliff top beside the road.

THE LOST LANDS OF LYONESSE, MOUNT'S BAY

Sunken lands, hidden beneath the constantly changing waters of the ocean surface are a part of many worldwide beliefs. The most famous inundation is included in the Bible as the story of Noah and the Ark, probably centred near Ur or Babylon, in the valley of the Tigris and Euphrates rivers. Celtic countries also have their own legends referring to sunken empires, with Wales claiming the existence of lands beneath Cardigan Bay, and Brittany, a sunken city. West Cornwall has the famous Lost Lands of Lyonesse.

The evidence underlying the legend of Lyonesse is based in geological fact, since Mount's Bay does have the remains of a submerged forest, near the Long Rock (SW499308), now a reef in the offshore bay. At very low tides, the petrified tree bases can be seen near the rock, several hundred yards from the shoreline. Indeed, the Cornish name for St Michael's Mount, Ictis, testifies to the translation 'Hoar rock in the wood'. This harks back several millennia to Neolithic times when the whole bay area, between Cudden

MOUNT'S BAY: This photograph was taken at a very high spring tide. Try to imagine the sea as a forest and St Michael's Mount standing up in the middle. Here may lie part of the Lost Lands of Lyonesse.

Point (SW548275) and Mousehole (SW473264) was a dense forest of oak, hazel and elder trees.

Mount's Bay forest was thought to be part of the legendary Lyonesse, now sunken beneath the waves, although haunting sounds coming from it are still heard, to this day. Lyonesse was once reputed to stretch almost 40 miles to the Isles of Scilly. The capital of this mystical land of legend was believed to centre on the Seven Stones reef, which had been a high rocky mountain, approximately 15 miles from Land's End.

Lyonesse might well have been in existence around 1500BC, since during the last Ice Age large animals such as sabre-toothed tigers, hairy mammoths and woolly rhinoceros crossed from the European mainland. They would have forded the wide river, which later became the English Channel, when the melt water from the ice sheets of the Ice Age flooded in, covering Lyonesse and its reputed 140 churches.

The final inundation of Lyonesse was said to have taken place one dreadful night, with just a single survivor who fled on a swift white horse, followed by the incoming tidal wave. His heroic survival, by reaching Perranuthnoe Sands (SW540292) and safety, led to the white horse being remembered in the heraldic shields of the Trevelyan and Vyvyan families, leaving some doubt as to the actual family to which the survivor belonged. Of course, the process of tidal inundation is more likely to have been a gradual event from the progressive rise of sea levels from the melt water. In Roman times there is a record of an Island of Ennor, protected from the sea by high sand dunes. This land was supposedly near the Isles of Scilly but was subject to frequent breaches of the dune barrier, as a result of marine surges.

The legend of Lyonesse has recently been supported by finds of pottery, bricks and other artefacts trawled up from the seabed around the Seven Stones lighthouse. Perhaps this classic Cornish legend is based on a true story from ancient times.

The Evidence

The existence of a submerged forest, as mentioned earlier, clearly illustrates that St Michael's Mount was once a high rocky hill surrounded by woodland. Some evidence of petrified tree stumps can be found in our local museums, as well as at the Long Rock during certain times of storm or very low tide. The submergence of this forest must have been at a date prior to the early Phoenician trade with the Mount for tin ore. This can be fixed approximately to the first millennium BC and, perhaps more accurately, to the third or fourth centuries BC. Reference is made in early records to the export centre of Ictis. St Michael's Mount is almost certainly the same place as this fabled land. The Mount must have already been a harbour and the surrounding bay fully flooded by the fourth century BC. This is roughly in keeping with a late-Neolithic inundation.

There is also a strong element of the supernatural in this story. The large number of churches supposedly existing on Lyonesse seems to have led to a peculiar modern-day phenomenon. Several visitors to the area, particularly close to Land's End, have claimed to hear phantom chimes emanating from underneath the waves, some distance away. Recently, a woman visiting Land's End, with no previous knowledge of tales about lost Lyonesse, heard the peals of a church bell, seemingly from an area well offshore. This witness is one of many who have heard these mysterious echoes and peals.

Stories of Lyonesse are amongst a number of Cornish elemental disasters, the most famous being the divine retribution supposedly called down on Langarrow, a great city situated in the extensive area of sand dunes stretching from Perranporth to Holywell Bay. Legends recount tales of a convict work-force during the Dark Ages (fifth to eighth centuries), used to build the city and widen the Gannel estuary. These 'undesirables' intermingled with local residents, thus lowering standards of family life and general morals. The Almighty, angered by the Cornish decline, swept up storms to move huge tracts of sand in a week-long tempest, in order to bury the new city.

As recently as the nineteenth century, shifting sands at Gwithian Towans (SW579411), near Hayle, uncovered an early church, whilst the former village of Lelant is thought to be under the waters of St Ives Bay, swamped by another marine inundation. Similarly church bells are sometimes heard coming from this spot in St Ives Bay.

Location

Mount's Bay itself stretches from Mousehole to Cudden Point and Prussia Cove and, as stated, holds the vast remains of the mixed forests said to form part of Lyonesse. At the Seven Stones reef, many ships have been wrecked including the *Torrey Canyon* in 1967, from which dreadful environmental pollution was unleashed on to the Cornish coastline. On a clear day, the Isles of Scilly are just visible from Land's End as a small black dot on the far horizon, beyond the Longships lighthouse. Many people think that the Isles of Scilly are part of the remains of a hill range, once the border of Lyonesse.

DEMON TREGEAGLE, LOE BAR, PORTHCURNO

Many claim that the infamous Jan Tregeagle is merely the personification of some ancient Celtic god, whose supposed activities were based in the Cornish peninsula. Tregeagle's wailing spectre is usually associated with some of the county's most remote, barren and inhospitable environments. In particular, Bodmin Moor has become the centre for many of his penances, where his tormented soul is forced to make amends for his evil life by means of an incredible range of impossible tasks.

There is little doubt that Jan did actually exist, not as a Celtic god but in the early-seventeenth century as an unpopular local magistrate, who abused his powers and committed several heinous crimes, including the murder of his wife and children. Tregeagle is reputed to have seized estates from an orphan child, and bribed the local clergy to bury his body in consecrated ground at St Breock church. But his ghost was soon summoned to suffer eternal punishment at various Cornish locations.

The legend of Tregeagle is long and confused, so if the reader will permit, the authors will concentrate on a small part of the story by limiting the tales to those hauntings of coastal areas in the south-west peninsula, only briefly referring to other legendary aspects of the whole Tregeagle story. Apparently, his spirit was called up as a witness during a disputed trial in Bodmin's court. To assist the defendant, Tregeagle testified to the court, but was not returned properly from whence he had been summoned.

Instead, local clergy were forced to bind the restless spirit and a series of punishments imposed on the hapless Tregeagle, designed to keep him busy for eternity. His spirit was firstly sent to Padstow Bay to weave sand ropes, which were then constantly destroyed by the incoming tide. Tregeagle's screams and moans of anger kept the locals awake and deeply uneasy. Then his spirit was relocated by St Petroc to remain within the borders of Penwith. At Berepper Sands near Helston, Tregeagle had to fill sacks with sand and then carry them over to Loe Bar Estuary, only to tip the contents at Porthleven. He was to be free once again as soon as Berepper became an area of flat rock, without sand. However, each tide brought back the sands to Berepper on the existing strong tidal flow.

One day a demon tripped Tregeagle whilst he was carrying loaded sand sacks across the estuary and it became blocked with what is now Loe Bar. Since the harbour at the Loe Estuary was now ruined, the locals were very angry, and Tregeagle was next sent to the Land's End region. Here at Porthcurno he was ordered to sweep the sand from its beautiful beach, and to cover the rocks at

LOE BAR AND POOL: According to legend this was once a natural harbour, silted up by the demon Tregeagle, forming a land-locked lake. Berepper Sands, where Lutey found Morvena the mermaid, begins on the extreme left of the picture.

Nanjizal (or Mill Bay). Storms inevitably returned it all on a regular basis and Tregeagle could be heard above the gales, bellowing in fury towards the cliff tops.

The Evidence

Tregeagle's ghost has been identified over past centuries at many inland locations, particularly Bodmin Moor and Roche Rock, although at coastal sites he is heard rather than seen above the rage of the storm. Although the ghost hunter may well smile at any suggestion that Tregeagle still exists, he or she may wish to stand on the cliffs beside Loe Bar or above Nanjizal Bay and listen to the range of sounds. These vary from the cries of wheeling seabirds to the thunder of Atlantic breakers. So, although Tregeagle is now surely just a legend, there are those who believe that the screams of this terrifying ghoul are heard in atrocious weather. At times of tempest, this sea-coast environment can assume a very dark and menacing mantle.

Location

Nanjizal (or Mill Bay) (SW355235) is featured in the 'Daisy Dog' story and can only be reached on foot. Porthcurno Cove, towards Land's End, is off the B3315 road and has a large car park at the head of the inlet (SW384225). It is a beauty spot well worth a visit at any season.

Loe Bar is approached from Porthleven by the cliff road (SW628257). Parking on the cliff is available in a limited area about half a mile from Porthleven. Access to Loe Bar can then be reached on foot along the cliffs where the in-filled estuary and ruined harbour once stood (SW643242).

These locations provide an interesting and challenging coastal walk for the energetic of all ages. Finally, 'evidence' of Tregeagle's sand-dumping exploits is visible from the cliffs above Pedn-Vounder Beach, adjacent to the Porthcurno Valley (SW394224). Here lie several enormous sand bars across

PEDN-VOUNDER BEACH: Here at low tide are seen Tregeagle's sand bars, which he must continually re-create as his penance to the end of time.

the entrance to this Atlantic beach. At certain tides, the bars regularly vanish and reappear at neighbouring locations along the cliff bases. It looks as if Tregeagle's punishment will almost certainly be for eternity!

Bibliography and Further Reference

Addicoat, Ian. *Ghost Hunting: A Tour of West Cornwall's Ghosts, Spirits and Hauntings*, 2000.

Addicoat, Ian. *Ghostly Tales Of Cornwall: For the 21st Century*, 2001.

Behenna, John. *Westcountry Shipwrecks: A Pictorial Record 1866–1973*, 1974.

Bottrell, William. *Traditions and Hearthside Stories* (vols 1,2,3), 1870–1880.

Cook, Judith. *Cornish Walks and Legends*, 1979.

Courtney, Margaret. *Cornish Feasts and Folklore*, 1890.

Du Maurier, Daphne. *Vanishing Cornwall*, 1967.

Francis, Di. *Cornish Ghosts*. 1977.

Graham, Frank. *Smuggling in Cornwall*. 1982.

Hirth, Eric. *Ghosts in Cornwall*. 1986.

Hunt, Robert. *Romance and Superstitions of the West of England*, 1881.

Ivey, W.F. *Wrecks Around our Coast*, 1981.

Jones, Kelvin I. *Penzance Customs and Superstitions*, 1997.

Maddison, Arthur. *The West Country's Maritime Story*, 1982.

Priestland, Gerald and Sylvia. *West of Hayle River*, 1980.

Pyatt, Edward C. *Cornwall Coast Path*, 1976.

Folklore, Myths and Legends of Britain. Reader's Digest Association Ltd., 1973.

Truran, Christine. *A Short Cornish Dictionary*, 1986.

Underwood, Peter. *Ghosts of Cornwall*, 1998.

Weatherhill, Craig. *Belerion: Ancient Sites of Land's End*, 1981.
Weatherhill, Craig, Devereux Paul. *Myths and Legends of Cornwall,* 1998.

White, Paul. *Classic West Country Ghost Stories.* 1996.
White, Paul. *Classic Cornish Ghost Stories.* 1999.

Williams, Michael. *Supernatural in Cornwall.* 1974.

MAPS:

Ordnance Survey – Explorer Map No.7 Land's End   1:25000
Ordnance Survey – Explorer Map No.8 The Lizard   1:25000